Teaching Information Technology 1 4

Teaching 14+

Series editor: Andy Armitage

Published and forthcoming titles:

Teaching Information Technology 14+

Jane Evershed and Jayne Roper

 Open University Press

Open University Press
McGraw-Hill Education
McGraw-Hill House
Shoppenhangers Road
Maidenhead
Berkshire
England
SL6 2QL

email: enquiries@openup.co.uk
world wide web: www.openup.co.uk

and Two Penn Plaza, New York, NY 10121–2289, USA

First published 2010

Copyright © Jane Evershed and Jayne Roper 2010

A catalogue record of this book is available from the British Library

ISBN-13: 978-0-33-523799-9 (pb) 978-0-33-523798-2 (hb)
ISBN-10: 0335237991 (pb) 0335237983 (hb)

Library of Congress Cataloging-in-Publication Data
CIP data has been applied for

Typeset by RefineCatch Limited, Bungay, Suffolk
Printed in the UK by Bell & Bain Ltd, Glasgow

Fictitious names of companies, products, people, characters and/or data that
may be used herein (in case studies or in examples) are not intended to
represent any real individual, company, product or event.

The **McGraw·Hill** Companies

Contents

List of figures

List of tables

Series editor's preface

For historical reasons perhaps, subject pedagogy for Post 16 teachers has not been considered a professional development priority. The possession of appropriate academic or vocational qualifications and experience have traditionally been considered sufficient for those teaching older students assumed themselves to possess the motivation and skills for effective learning. However, the increasing numbers of 14–16 year olds taking part of their programmes in FE colleges, the rise in the participation rate of 16–19 year olds and the increasing number of 18–30 year olds having experience of higher education, have created a large and diverse population in all sector institutions presenting a challenge to those teaching Post 14 students. Both the 2003 and 2006 Ofsted surveys of Post 16 teacher training and the 2007 reforms of initial teacher training and continuing professional development, have drawn attention to the urgent need for both new and existing teachers to receive training to teach their subject or curriculum specialism and to receive support from subject coaches or mentors in the workplace. Most of the programmes preparing the 40,000 trainees annually to teach in the lifelong learning sector are generic in nature, rather than subject specific.

Partly because of the Institute for Learning's requirements regarding both CPD and professional formation, there is considerable growth in in-service continuing professional development and, given the attention given by both Ofsted and DCSF to subject pedagogy as described above, it is likely that there will be a sharp CPD focus for many colleges on subject teaching, particularly since much of the burden of subject based training will fall on the shoulders of FE college based mentors. The increase in vocational education in schools, particularly with the introduction of diplomas, will see a growing need for secondary PGCE students and existing 14–18 secondary teachers to enhance their subject pedagogy for 14+ students. One of the key recommendations of a recent report on vocational teacher training[1] is that "Vocational and applied pedagogies should become a research priority and be embedded within school, further education (FE) and higher education (HE) initial teacher training (ITT) and continuing professional development (CPD)."

[1] The Skills Commission (2010) *An Inquiry into Teacher training in Vocational Education* London: The Skills Commission P.14

Each series title is therefore aimed to act as support for teachers, whether on a formal initial or CPD programme or simply as a guide for those teaching the subject on a daily basis in one of a variety of possible contexts: secondary, FE, Adult and Community Education, work-based training. Chapters in each title follow a similar format. Chapter 1 deals with the nature of subject(s) in the curriculum area, considering any contesting conceptions of what the subject should be about, as well as current issues connected with teaching it. There is a focus on subject updating, identifying recent key developments in subjects as well as the means for students to be able to update themselves. Chapter 2 provides an introduction to the major programmes in the subject area focussing mainly on those in the National Qualifications Framework such as GCSE, AS, Key Skills, NVQ, Diplomas, although reference is made to the Framework for Higher Education Qualifications. There is a consideration of the central features of each programme such as aims and objectives, unitisation or modularity, content. The chapter also guides readers in the task of turning syllabus into learning via schemes of work. The third chapter considers key skills and functional skills, looking at differing models of skills development and how such skills might be taught through the subject. Chapter 4 looks at the teaching and learning strategies most often used in the curriculum area. There are clearly certain learning and teaching strategies that are used universally across post 14 programmes – lectures, discussion, presentations are the most obvious. Even these, however, will need to be treated in the context of their use in the subject area. Presentations which model those in advertising or marketing might be effective learning strategies in an AS Media Studies or Applied Business GCSE, whereas in Key Skills Communications they might have the purpose of developing oracy skills and as part of an Access course of developing study skills. Chapter 5 considers resources as used in the context of the curriculum area. When audio-visual resources are being considered, for example, students might be presented with exemplar handouts and PowerPoint presentations with subject-related content. ICT resources should be considered in terms of their strengths in relation to the subject. Are there good commercial software packages, for example? How can they best be used for teaching? What are the key web sites relating to the subject area? How might searching best be carried out? There is a consideration of the range of published resources available in the subject area, with examples of how material is presented and how use of it is structured. Chapter 6 offers guidance on the role of the teacher as assessor in the programmes identified in Chapter 2, with a particular emphasis on the range of assessment strategies used as part of these programmes.

Each title features a range of pedagogical features which might be useful alone, in pairs or in groups. Readers are invited for example to reflect, discuss, respond to a range of visual stimuli, give short answer responses to questions, consider case studies, complete short tasks.

Jane Evershed and Jayne Roper describe how information technology has permeated our everyday lives since the 1980s and note key features of this growth such as the gender imbalance in usage and the existence of 'digital natives' and 'digital immigrants'. The central driver of this growth is the explosion in use of the internet with some 1668.8 million users worldwide and a 75% penetration in developed countries such as the UK, USA and Germany. Traditionally, IT teaching and training has been regarded as relatively narrowly instructional, offering a 'how to' guide. However, the authors demonstrate the wide range of pedagogical methods available to the IT teacher, as well as to teachers embedding IT-based technologies in their teaching of other subjects (Information Learning Technology or ILT). In addition, a very broad range of differing types of IT qualifications exists. Not that the authors regard the end product or qualification as the most important aspect of learning in IT but defend the subject's intrinsic worth.

Andy Armitage

Acknowledgements

We would like to thank everyone who has supported us in creating this book and our family, friends and colleagues from whom we continue to learn. Special thanks to Andy, Billie, Colin, Lou, Olivia, Paul and Peter for their help and advice.

We dedicate this book to David and Jeff, without whose support the research for this book would still be sitting on the kitchen table.

1

Current issues in information technology

In this chapter we will focus on:

- What IT means today in the UK and the importance of the IT industry and its associated infrastructure.
- Some of the impacts that IT has on culture and society in terms of the digital divide, security issues and access to technology.
- How **internet** technologies offer the potential for global and local economic interaction and social inclusion.
- Recent government policy initiatives, including the report on Digital Britain.
- Copyright ethics of internet and other sources accessed through IT media.

Introduction

What is information technology (IT) and what is its role in society? Is it important and, if so, why?

These are very complex questions to which we suggest no one has the definitive answers. However, it is essential for teachers of IT disciplines to recognize that understanding such questions is vital for teaching the subject. It is very easy to be drawn into 'teaching to the exam' and to launch into creating product-based assessments that many of the IT qualifications advocate. How often, ourselves included, have teachers taken the syllabus, divided it up into schemes of work and found that the criteria have been so wide in scope and the timetable in which to deliver it has been so tight that we have launched into new subjects without fully explaining or allowing our students – of whatever age – to first explore the concepts involved. We argue throughout this book that it is this part of the teaching and learning process that creates the initial sparks of interest and that, by chaining ourselves to producing end products we may be successful in helping students to gain specific qualifications, but that for interest to continue we also need to harness those initial sparks and keep them alight.

Chapter 1 starts the process of unravelling some of the pertinent issues in IT today by identifying some of the main IT disciplines, where they might be found in everyday life and the impacts they can have on a broad range of societal issues, including education, ethics, economics and culture.

The debates are extended in Chapter 2 as some of the rapidly changing features of the sector are investigated, including the emerging trends in IT, the role of IT in the green agenda and the changes in employment patterns that rapidly changing convergent and divergent technologies can enable.

In Chapter 3 the importance of industry experience and the importance of 'keeping it real' within teaching are highlighted. The relevance of continuing professional development (**CPD**) to model modern work practices for students is discussed.

Some of the issues within the IT world are analysed in Chapter 4, for example the gender imbalance and digital divide between 'digital natives' and 'digital immigrants', and preparing students for work through placements and apprenticeships.

Chapter 5 contains an overview of IT qualifications from entry level to above level 4, including summary tables of example qualifications and awarding bodies.

In Chapter 6 we examine some of the prevalent learning and teaching pedagogies in IT and open the debate as to how IT is viewed in society: as a set of functional skills or as the start of a journey towards creating a knowledge society. We discuss health and safety issues, equality and diversity.

In Chapter 7 some of the IT resources available to teachers of IT are discussed. There are examples of blended and project-based teaching and learning strategies to interest and motivate across a wide age and ability range. We demonstrate how some popular IT resources can be harnessed to good effect for teaching IT and other programmes.

Finally, in Chapter 8, the debate on how IT is viewed in society is revisited through its use in assessment. The relative merits of diagnostic and initial assessments are discussed, along with the importance of the assessment for learning reforms in formative assessment strategies. Suggestions are included on methods for group and **e-assessment** along with inclusive strategies and the need to maintain quality and reliability.

IT in everyday life

The term IT has shifted and developed rapidly since the 1980s, coinciding with a time of technological miniaturization of the chip from mainframe computers to the now ubiquitous personal computer (**PC**) and laptop equipment. During the past two decades or so, electronic devices have become smaller and converged functionally into increasingly powerful and more portable devices, and have integrated into society often so seamlessly (despite the occasional grumble about speed!) that we do not even realize we are using IT; we adjust our central heating, withdraw money from a cash machine and buy groceries from a supermarket without thinking of the IT industry that services and supports such activities.

Reflection 1.1

Make a list of the IT you have used today as you went about your normal day. For example, you may have listened to digital radio or put petrol in your car. Then reflect on which of these seemingly local interactions may have more global impacts.

One example you may have investigated is ordering a book online from a website, which could be located anywhere in the world. Web pages can be saved on globally distributed servers and could mean you placing your order from an overseas company. You are likely to receive an e-mail notification that your order has been placed; again Internet Service Providers (**ISP**) use multiple communication links including satellite to route your order and e-mail communication. In all probability, your book will be dispatched and tracked by electronic means, electronic stock control will be used, and it is likely that the publisher will be notified and royalties calculated automatically via the internet. The website through which you ordered the book will update the profile it holds of you so it can recommend additional titles based on your previous purchases. The payment will be made electronically using a credit or debit card. The fee will be deducted and the transaction made between your bank and the international bank of the supplier, all online via the internet.

Behind the easy façade of such transactions there are legions of people employed in the IT industry. There are specialists and generalists in multiple disciplines including software programming, hardware configuration and design, network management, business analysis, web design, database analysis and games testing. There are product innovators, manufacturers and designers. There are marketing companies, advertisers, journals and magazines all specializing in IT. There are IT security companies, computer repair and support companies, IT peripheral suppliers and manufacturers, and IT retailers. The list is endless. And IT is no longer just about computers, it involves information and communications technologies (**ICT**) such as mobile phones, Voice over internet Protocol (**VoIP**), **Twitter, Facebook** and e-mail networks, information learning technologies (**ILT**) such as virtual learning environments (**VLE**) and interactive whiteboard systems, music and entertainment, games and other highly specialized systems such as those designed for air traffic control and the stock market, for example. Other huge industries rely in turn on IT, for example, retailing, banking and the tracking of goods and services. IT is a vast web of interconnections (and sometimes frustratingly non-interconnected systems) often (thankfully) obscured and opaque to the end user. All of this is made global through copper, fibre optic, wireless and satellite networks.

Employment in the sector

Even in the global recession **E-Skills UK**, the Sector Skills Council for Business and Information Technology, reported:

Though the jobs market looked pretty bleak during Q1.09, it is worth mentioning that the number of ICT staff in work during the first quarter of the year was still

4 per cent higher than the equivalent quarter of 2008 (compared with a 1 per cent fall for the UK workforce as a whole).

(E-Skills UK 2009a)

Case Study 1.1

A large insurance company with 1000 employees has very different IT needs from a large doctor's surgery, but there is also some overlap. The insurance company will have a call centre for enquiries, and the receptionists at the surgery perform a very similar function. The calls are likely to be logged into a database in both cases (though the front end may well look very different) and both will rely on voice and telephony. From Table 1.1, identify which IT personnel may be required by each business and whether they are likely to be required on-site or whether they are more likely to be outsourced from elsewhere.

Table 1.1   List of IT personnel who may be required by different companies

IT personnel	Doctor's surgery	Insurance company
Voice and telephony support to ensure telephone and voice communication is maintained	*Outsourced*	*On site*
IT help desk to support staff when IT problems are encountered		
Technical support to assist with software and hardware issues and implement changes to IT systems		
Network support to install network infrastructure and solve network problems		
Software developers to create new software programs and applications		
Business analysts to determine efficiencies and improvements to IT systems		
Back-up managers to ensure data is safe and retrievable		
IT trainers to train new staff and improve efficiency		
IT asset managers to ensure that IT equipment is accounted for, maintained, repaired and updated		
Research and development personnel to create new innovative products and services		
IT project manager to oversee changes to IT systems in a planned and systematic fashion and perhaps design policies for the use of such systems		

Most of the IT functions will be required by both the insurance and doctor's surgery, but the mode of delivery will be very different. For the surgery most of the services will be outsourced through the parent company, in this case the National Health Service. The insurance company is more likely to have on-site IT professionals, though the trend towards outsourcing help desks is still in fashion. Ireland, Scotland and India have large numbers of call centre based help desks.

To begin to truly understand what IT is, we need to be able to connect what we do locally with what is happening globally, to look behind the easy, user-friendly devices we take for granted to the more global, all-pervading sides of IT to recognize and understand how IT impacts on all our lives in Western society and how it directly and indirectly affects even the poorest individuals in underdeveloped economies. IT has the means to change employment patterns, transform industry and commerce and provide opportunities to communicate and participate within and between communities. IT both services and drives economies. The disadvantage is that it also has the potential to divide and fragment society, marginalize and corrupt. IT is an all-pervading invention that is a reflection of our culture, desires, aspirations and human frailties. Its multitude of applications reflect the best and the worst that society is capable of, and that is the subject of further debate in Chapters 3 and 4.

The rise of the internet

The main driver of IT change in society, culture and commerce has been the explosion in internet use. Since Berners-Lee invented the hypertext transfer protocols (**HTTP**) that enable the distribution of hypertext resources on the World Wide Web (**WWW**), the compilation of collaborative and **hypermedia** information that is generally available has expanded exponentially.

With a world population in 2009 estimated at 6767.8 million and some 1668.8 million users globally, this is close to a 25 per cent penetration rate. This rapid escalation in internet penetration is perhaps best demonstrated by the figures in Table 1.2, showing percentage increases in internet users against head of population.

It is interesting to note from Table 1.2 that the US, Germany and the UK all have similar penetration rates of around 75 per cent of the population; although these countries still have some new-to-market customers to target, much of the internet

Table 1.2 Percentage growth in internet users and penetration, 2002–2009

Country	User growth 2000–2009 (%)	Internet penetration rate, 2009 (%)	Estimated population, 2009 (millions)	Estimated number of internet users, 2009 (millions)
US	145.8	76.3	307.2	234.4
UK	203.1	76.4	61.1	46.7
Germany	158.2	75.5	82.3	62.0
China	1606.7	28.7	1338.6	384.0
India	1520.0	7.0	1156.9	81.0

Source: http://internetworldstats.com, September 2009.

market is saturated in these more IT mature countries. Global marketing campaigns are now firmly geared towards countries such as India and China where penetration rates are much lower and where potential growth is much greater, the number of potential new internet users in each of these countries being around a billion. This is graphically displayed in Figure 1.1.

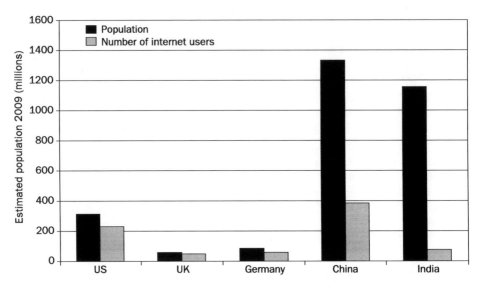

Figure 1.1 Potential growth in the number of internet users, 2009
Source: http://internetworldstats.com, September 2009.

Despite the number of internet users in China already being more than the number of users in the US, UK and Germany combined, these countries are seen as the major growth areas by global industry and commerce for the next decade due to their large populations. This is not lost on countries such as China and India as they gear up to producing highly skilled IT professionals, technologists and designers to complement their already widespread peripheral industries, including call and service centres.

IT Security

Infrastructure damage

As the reliance on the internet increases, the protection of the infrastructure becomes vital. This was demonstrated in 2008 when earthquakes in the Mediterranean damaged undersea cables and many thousands of individuals and businesses were left without internet access.

There are over 100 submarine cable routes criss-crossing the oceans and seas, carrying internet and voice data around the world. In the UK a major location for landfall of these cables is Cornwall; in India it is around Mumbai, and in America there are a considerable number of cables making landfall near New York. Most of the cables are in deep water, but there are some major bottlenecks where cables are squeezed between landmasses such as in the Mediterranean Sea and they are vulnerable at these points and at landfall locations. The surprisingly delicate undersea cables are laid across the sea floor and are prone to damage by ships' anchors and natural disasters such as earthquakes. There is increasing concern that they are also vulnerable to terrorist attack. Internet blackouts can cause huge economic damage.

In 2005 independent research by the Swiss Federal Institute of Technology (Mi2G 2005) quantified the economic impact of an internet blackout affecting the whole of Switzerland for one week. The researchers forecasted damage to the economy at 1.2 per cent of gross domestic product. In Switzerland, 48 per cent of all 3.59 million jobs were classified as being IT intensive, a percentage similar to most of the G8 member countries.

Reflection 1.2

What would be the effect of a one-week internet blackout on the economy of the UK or on your educational establishment, workplace or home?

You may have identified productivity losses and revenue losses quite readily, but what about the cost of repairs, the loss of data, and any liabilities from not completing transactions or the loss of customers as they use alternative sites?

Losing data

Frequently identified causes of data security compromises are losing equipment, inadequate security or hardware failure, lack of adequate back-up procedures, **viruses** and identity fraud. Table 1.3 lists some more examples. Hardware failure or damage can have substantial impacts on business and on personal life. Imagine losing all the information on your memory stick, or all your lesson planning and teaching resources, registers, school records, timetabling and reports that are saved at work being destroyed if the main network server is damaged by fire or flood. The impact would be devastating. Taking regular data back-ups is essential to ensure that the impact is minimized through mirroring of hard disks, where information is stored on two separate hard disks simultaneously, or duplicating data onto a portable hard drive that can be locked in a fireproof safe. Data on memory sticks can be backed up by saving the information on a hard drive as well as on the portable device. There is also an expanding IT market in providing disaster recovery for emergency planning scenarios where companies are contracted to back up data and provide ready-made premises for companies to relocate to in the event of an emergency.

Reflection 1.3

Can you identify how you minimize the risk of losing data in your own teaching practice? What steps do you or can you take to minimize or reduce the impact or risk of this occurring?

Table 1.3 Potential data compromises and potential ways to reduce impacts

Compromise	To minimize impact
Data loss – physical, e.g. loss of a laptop, memory stick, CD	Encrypt data, use password protection, implement rigorous data back-up procedures, minimize the number of copies of data, implement strict policies on data sharing
Data loss – data corruption, e.g. viruses, hard-drive or portable drive failure or damage	Implement rigorous data back-up procedures, install firewalls, use virus checker, minimize sharing of portable data devices
Hacking – where a person can gain access to the information on your computer, usually by gaining administrative passwords	Install firewalls, secure wireless networks, implement user access control, restrict physical access to equipment and cabling, change passwords regularly and remember to log off correctly
Phishing – where identity theft is typically perpetrated through e-mails purporting to be from a bank or trusted supplier and requesting sensitive information such as bank or card details and passwords	Use spam filters and junk mail identifiers, do not open any unrecognized e-mails, never give your full password to anyone, and consider setting unusual answers to security questions, e.g. place of birth – set at something other than your real birthplace
Undesirable material	Install access controls, spam and firewall filters
E-safety	Teach students e-safety, especially relevant on social networking sites, e-mails and chat rooms

Identity theft

There have been several recent cases in the news of personal data being compromised after government officials have lost laptops or sent unencrypted data CDs in the post. Table 1.3 indicates some of the potential issues concerned with unsecured data and suggested strategies that may help to minimize any damage caused. Such losses of data can compromise both national and personal security. The use of biometrics, such as iris and fingerprint scanning, to authenticate identity in IT brings with it serious concerns over civil rights and personal freedom, although advances in this new generation of software are being made continually and face and behaviour recognition facilities are currently being tested by the security industry.

With more of the world's population using the internet, we have opened ourselves up to a new type of fraud – online fraud. This can appear in many guises; but one increasingly prevalent method is known as **phishing**. Unsolicited e-mails are received by individuals from what appears to be your own bank or credit card company. Some of these are obviously fraudulent as you can recognize that they are not from your bank and should be left unopened and sent directly to your junk e-mail. However, others appear very authentic and explain (falsely) that your details have been compromised and that to rectify the situation you should follow the internet site link given in the e-mail and type in your password and account details. If you were to follow these instructions, you would end up victim to a scam designed to extract details from you to allow someone else access to your accounts. Other scams include fraudsters surreptitiously installing malware (malicious software) onto a computer to track which sites users access and then records the credentials needed in order to gain access to their personal pages (including, for example, internet banking, e-mail, social networking and remote corporate access).

With each technological advance comes a new raft of risk factors and potentials for data loss, intrusion and theft. The recent upsurge in wireless technology in educational establishments, commercial enterprises and in the home has led to security breaches through the interception of electronically transmitted information (such as internet traffic or phone calls). However, this risk needs to be balanced against the convenience of using **WiFi** hotspots (wireless access points) in cafés and other public areas. Many home users with wireless access have unused bandwidth and are happy to share this with others. It is not unusual in many urban areas to find that your home already has wireless internet availability from several or perhaps dozens of neighbouring properties. Some home owners prefer to security-enable their networks and restrict access to authorized users only. Others, usually in more rural areas, are willing to share unused bandwidth with anyone within signal range, on a reciprocal basis. Thus a whole community's internet coverage can be served by the connections of a few dozen altruistic individuals.

However, we would not want to invite just anyone to use our wireless internet connection, in much the same way as we would not invite just anyone to deposit unidentified items in our garden shed or take a suitcase on board a plane for the very nice person we just met at the airport. Nice as it would be to share our free wireless capacity, such generosity could perhaps be viewed as a little careless, and we may end up having to convince police that we really did not use our connection to download unsuitable images from the internet last week. However, there are new products becoming available, and one to look out for is Free Open Network (**FON**) from British Telecom. Essentially FON is a facility to give others the opportunity to share your unused bandwidth; it provides a **firewall** that prevents other users from hacking into your network and allows your traffic to take precedence over others.

Reflection 1.4

Consider the repercussions of someone being able to access your personal data. What would be the consequences? Do you take student information home on a laptop or memory stick? What steps do you take to minimize or reduce the impact or risk of these events occurring?

Reflection 1.5

Familiarize yourself with the legislation on data security, including the Computer Misuse Act (1990) and the Data Protection Act (1998).

Copyright ethics

Most readers were hopefully taught from a young age the difference between right and wrong. Most would consider themselves to be law-abiding citizens and shun the pursuit of illegal activities. But how many have copied a CD or DVD for a friend, photocopied sheet music or pages from books or used illegal copies of software, either knowingly or unknowingly? Many do not associate copying a computer game or CD with piracy, but according to the law, those who do this are just as guilty as the person selling stolen goods outside the local pub.

As we have become increasingly digitally acute, attitudes towards **downloading** have changed. Many areas concerned with downloading have altered dramatically over the last 20 years on a global scale related to the publishing, music and film industries. Access to ever increasing broadband speeds has meant that we are now able to download an entire DVD in less than three minutes. When this ease of down-loading is married with the portability of music, film and books, it is easy for copyright infringements to occur or for copyright to be simply ignored.

During the 1990s, there were peer-to-peer file sharing sites that one could join in order to download music and films without charge. These sites, needless to say, cared nothing about the copyright associated with each file, and members were able to upload files of their own as a contribution to the files available, again, with no regard to copyright. Courts of law around the world came down on the side of the film and music industries, meaning that these sites had to get 'cleaned up'.

The issues surrounding the copyright of literary material and music are broadly similar, but there are some differences. The important difference of principle is that all those individuals involved in creating a sound recording are entitled to be paid for the sale, broadcasting and public performance of the work. Therefore performers as well as composers can derive income from the sale, performance or broadcasting of sound recordings. By international law the copyright for performers is generally limited to 50 years from the date of the recording's first release. This means that any recording published or released to the public before 1960 is now out of copyright and therefore in the public domain. The copyright for written material belongs to the author and publisher. In UK law, literary material is protected by copyright which expires 70 years after the end of the calendar year in which the author dies. However, if the work is of unknown authorship, copyright expires 70 years after the end of the calendar year in which the work was created or made available to the public.

Because of the availability of music sharing sites on the internet, music piracy has soared in recent years, to the extent that legislation has been enacted or is planned in many European countries and US states to protect the rights of composers and performers and to penalize illegal sharers and downloaders. The distribution of copyright material without permission through peer-to-peer networks and over the internet, is against the law in the UK. It may also be in breach of a downloader's contractual terms with ISPs.

Under UK law copyright material sent over the internet or stored on web servers will generally be protected in the same way as material in other media. Anyone wish-ing to distribute copyright-protected material over the internet should ensure that they have the permission of the owners of rights in the material unless copyright exceptions apply. Exceptions to copyright are, for example, if the material is to be · used for limited educational purposes.

Music downloads

With the portability of music having expanded further into products such as mobile phones, the demand for downloads has increased accordingly and, since the legalities have been more clearly laid out, we now have a wide range of legal options for purchasing music downloads.

Reflection 1.6

Discuss in small groups if you have ever downloaded music from the internet. Did you do this from a reputable site? How did you pay for it? How and where did you listen to the music? How many devices did you put the music tracks onto?

Any discussion around Reflection 1.6 on the subject of music downloads must liken a 'paid for' track to a legally purchased CD or to legally purchased software. If you own a CD, you can take it with you and play it on any compatible machine anywhere in the world. You are free to loan it to other people but you are not authorized to copy it and distribute it to others. Some of the major contenders in this downloading market at present are **iTunes, Amazon** and Play. From these sites you purchase on a track-by-track basis. Few purchasers now buy a whole album at once. These downloaded tracks can then be played on an MP3 player, on a mobile phone, on a computer or any wireless or USB compatible music system, just like the traditional and legal CD.

Other systems exist where people subscribe to a music database and pay a set fee for the privilege of downloading from them. Even classical music from past centuries has to be paid for because the performers of the music derive an income from such tracks. Examples of monthly subscription sites include **Kazaa, Napster** and Nokia Music Store. Some of these systems limit the number of devices that one can access the tracks from, although the device can be changed periodically.

E-book downloads

The **e-book** market has started to follow a similar trend to the music industry in terms of availability of downloads, following the invention of the electronic book reader. There are many printed books which no longer carry copyright (for example, any work published before 1923). These works are available for anyone to put into a suitable format to be read using an **e-reader** of some description without copyright infringement worries and often without payment. New works and those which are still under copyright, however, usually require payment for the author and publisher and will come under modern copyright laws.

On 19 November 2009 a settlement was reached between authors and publishers and **Google Books** (Google Books 2009), which had been accused of infringing copyright by scanning books and creating an electronic database in the US. The agreement classifies e-books into three categories, depending on whether they are in or out of print and whether they are in or out of copyright. However, according to Bunz (2009), **Google** has been ordered by the French courts to stop digitizing books and pay a daily fine of €10,000 until it removes extracts taken from French books from its online database.

Reflection 1.7

Look up the specifics of the court case (Google Books, 2009). Do you agree with the settlement that was reached? What are the three categories of books outlined in the agreement? List three positive consequences for the consumer, Google Books and the author or publisher from this agreement.

Other major online book retailers such as Waterstone's, WH Smith and Amazon also offer an e-book option from the internet. Such purchases offer a more immediate delivery than waiting for the retailer to deliver the book to you. The purchaser does need to be aware, however, that at present the e-readers use different file formats so it is essential to ensure that your e-reader is compatible. The e-reader has begun to revolutionize our libraries too, with forward-thinking councils such as Essex, Hatfield, Croydon and Bedfordshire offering e-books for library members. The system works on the 'limited use' system, where files are no longer usable after a set period of time, much like returning a physical book back to the lending library before the due date.

However, the issues with e-books continue after they have been bought and read. If we purchase a copy of a newly published book from a high-street bookshop, we are free to dispose of it as we see fit when we have finished with it; we may lend it to others, we may sell it as a second-hand book, we may give it to another person, or we may simply throw it away. E-books are discussed further in Chapter 2.

Reflection 1.8

Discuss how we should treat our e-books after we have read them. What are the choices that are available to us? What would you like to be able to do with them?

We all need to be aware of the issues surrounding downloads – unless from a reputable site, offers which seem too good to be true probably are! The music industry has clamped down heavily on sites such as **YouTube** where individuals were **uploading** music and videos without regard to copyright; YouTube has removed many unauthorized versions of film and music. In the digital age, respect needs to be developed in previously free and easy areas. As more and more people use these methods to gain access to digital downloads, prices of files and devices will decrease and yet the publisher, authors and performers still need an incentive to continue to create new works.

Towards a digital Britain

The digital divide

The term 'digital divide' has been in common usage since the late 1990s to describe the perceived polarization in society between those deemed to be 'digitally enabled' and those who are 'digitally excluded'. The divide is often discussed in terms of the technological divide between Third World countries and so-called 'developed' economies which are more able to harness IT for wealth creation. However, this divide is also replicated within developed economies where some can gain ready access to IT technology and education and others are less able to do so.

Reflection 1.9

Do you agree with this last statement? Reflect on how access to IT technologies and education has helped you in teaching and learning and how its absence may impact on others. Perhaps extend your ideas globally as well as locally.

Closing the gap

Current government policy in Britain is based on a firm belief that the divide is present and that its continuance will have negative impacts on both wealth creation and social cohesion. In 2007, it set up the Home Access Taskforce through Becta (formerly known as the British Educational Communications and Technology Agency) to consider a technology-related learner entitlement to close the gap for disadvantaged learners and enable home access for all school-aged children in England. It was later discussed as part of the Department for Children, Schools and Families (**DCSF**) *Children's Plan* which stated:

> There are significant educational benefits associated with having access to technology at home . . . [it] gives learners greater choice about where, when and how they study. Research shows that this helps to motivate learners and improve attainment . . . [and] can serve as a focal point for parents to become more actively involved in their child's education. This collaboration between learner and parent can further enhance a pupil's engagement and their achievement . . . At the moment there are over a million children with no access to a computer in the home. These children are disproportionately from disadvantaged backgrounds, and their limited access to technology reinforces attainment gaps.
>
> (DCSF 2007, p. 76)

In June 2008 Becta published the revised *Harnessing Technology Strategy* aimed at narrowing the gap between those with and without home access to technology. The core vision aims to provide access to learning beyond the confines of the school day, to increase opportunities for learning independently and to develop the skills needed to participate within communities and the technologically connected world with their family. This has resulted in a cultural shift in education pedagogies for both teachers and students.

> **Reflection 1.10**
>
> What pedagogic and cultural changes can you identify with the home access strategy? What barriers can you identify and how could they be overcome?

The *Independent Review of ICT User Skills* (Department for Business, Innovation and Skills (BIS) 2009b) by Baroness Estelle Morris extends the concepts of the *Harnessing Technology* report to the wider community, maintaining the link between access to the internet and economic and social welfare, stating: 'Digital skills have an impact on an adult's equality of access to information and services, employability, social inclusion, engagement in further learning, and on wider business productivity' (BIS 2009b, p. 6). The report uses the term 'digital life skill' to define 'the set of basic ICT skills an adult will require to take their first steps online' (BIS 2009b, p. 5). Morris recommended an 'entitlement' of 9 hours of basic skills training in IT for adults, mirroring other skills for life entitlements in numeracy and literacy. There has been a mixed reaction to such proposals, with some welcoming the re-emergence of funding for basic IT education for adults, while others see this as a narrowing of IT courses for adults to those which focus exclusively on the acquisition of internet skills. This debate is revisited in Chapter 4.

Digital expansion

Morris's report was published in tandem with the long awaited government report on *Digital Britain* written by Lord Stephen Carter (BIS 2009a), which sets out the government's vision of technology in Britain for the next decade. According to the report: 'In the last decade the number of adults who are online has increased from 8.1 million to 33.4 million. Yet 11 million adults in England are still ICT illiterate and meeting their needs is a considerable challenge' (BIS 2009a, p. 3). This statement would suggest that in order to be IT literate a person simply needs to be online. There are many who would suggest that just being able to surf the internet does not equate to being IT literate. There are many who believe it involves knowledge of software applications, an ability to troubleshoot simple hardware problems, to apply critical thinking to the plethora of information that populates the internet, and general **e-safety** awareness, and this is expanded upon further in Chapter 4.

The report sets out a government strategy for a universal broadband service to ensure that virtually every household will be able to access a broadband line capable of delivering at least 2 megabits per second (Mbps) by 2012. According to the report, the government recognizes the potential for digital technology to transform work and learning patterns through increasingly flexible working hours and **e-learning**. This is discussed further in Chapter 2.

Internet access is, however, only one strand of the large 245-page document that makes up the *Digital Britain* report. Much of it is concerned with copyright of intellectual property and the digital distribution of media bandwidth following the

2012 switch-over to digital broadcasting. The report outlines plans to sell the capacity to commercial and community operators for the provision of educational and community content. This has potentially enormous impacts on how education is delivered in schools and colleges as digital participation rises.

Summary of Key Points

- IT has profound impacts not only on economic welfare but also on social and cultural aspects of society.
- The constantly shifting technologies mean that IT teachers will need to keep their skills up to date to take advantage of any new technology and to advise students on opportunities and qualifications in IT.
- The main driver for change in the last 10 years has been the rise of the internet, especially in wireless technology. Teachers of IT need to teach not only the syllabus but also a general awareness of internet security.
- Government policy is directed towards the commercialization of digital broadcasting channels and increasing access to the internet for e-commerce and e-learning.

Useful website

Statistics on internet use are freely available at sites such as http://www.internetworldstats.com and can be utilized to embed numeracy into the IT curriculum.

Further reading

Intellectual Property Office (2009) What is peer to peer file sharing, and why does it affect copyright? http://www.ipo.gov.uk/types/copy/c-other/c-other-faq/c-other-faq-gen/c-other-faq-gen-peer.htm (accessed 20 December 2009).

Norris, P. (2001) *Digital Divide, Civic Engagement, Information Poverty and the internet Worldwide*. Cambridge: Cambridge University Press.

Van Dijk, J. (2005) *The Deepening Divide: Inequality in the Information Society*. London: Sage Publications.

2

Features of the sector

In this chapter we will focus on:

- The ubiquitous nature of IT.
- Current trends in IT and ICT.
- The green agenda.

When we are introducing ourselves it is usual for us to mention what line of work we are in. Everyone nods understandingly when we say that we are teachers and then, inevitably, they enquire which subject it is that we teach. If we were to reply 'English' we may raise a few smiles or 'I always liked English at school'; if we respond that we teach maths, we may be met with frowns and 'I've never been much good at maths' – but what is the reaction when we explain that we teach IT? The effect that this reply has on people is somewhat mixed. Some people think that they understand what this means, while others look completely blank. This should not come as a surprise to us as the area of IT is so vast and can mean so many different things. In a way we are lucky that our subject is constantly changing because we will have no fear of becoming bored with teaching the same material year after year.

It is currently estimated by the Office for National Statistics that 65 per cent of British households have a computer with access to the internet (see http://www.statistics.gov.uk), and many more people have access through internet cafés or public libraries (where the service is sometimes free). This new tool can be utilized by both teachers and students to facilitate a more flexible learning experience.

The ubiquitous nature of IT

Air is all around us and is necessary for continued living, and it seems that IT is all around us too, appearing in more and more places. We are all aware of the IT in the desktop computer or laptop, and most people would agree that any item which can be plugged into a computer would be classed as IT – but what are these things and what about the rest of our world?

Reflection 2.1

How do you use IT in your everyday life? What items do you have in your home and workplace which make use of IT? Is there anything that you do not use to its full capacity?

The term 'information and communication technology' (ICT) seems very vague, and there are many varied definitions if you look in different dictionaries. It is also easy to view any technology as ICT. Nevertheless, ICT is creeping into almost all areas of our lives at an amazing rate.

Many schools are using now personal digital assistants (**PDAs**) in place of paper registers. As each student enters the classroom they have their fingerprints scanned and an electronic register is sent back to the administration offices. This enables the school to quickly alert parents/carers to any truancy. This system has been extended to make some schools a cash-free zone. Parents/carers can put money into their child's account at school, and lunch money is deducted from the account via the fingerprint scanning method at the pay point of the canteen. Whilst the cash-free society in schools can reduce bullying, it does mean that if the system fails for any reason all of the monies in all of the accounts could be lost or altered. The school must have a secure mode of transfer for data over their network when dealing with personal and financial data and must ensure compliance with the Data Protection Act (refer back to the discussion of IT security in Chapter 1).

The prevalence of closed-circuit television (**CCTV**) security cameras, linked to IT networks, is controversial: there are those who feel that CCTV contributes to a safer society, and those who believe that civil rights are compromised by them. CCTV surveillance is seen by some as a way of making public spaces safer, but the vast majority of such spaces are not staffed or recorded at sufficient resolution. Cameras in town centres do not necessarily prevent crime, but can stop it from happening in the vicinity of the cameras and can help divert police officers to trouble spots. New-generation software is being introduced with face-recognition facilities that will automatically detect 'strange' behaviour or particular faces in a crowd based on biometrics. However, many civil rights groups have expressed concern that allowing continual increases in government surveillance will create a mass surveillance society, with minimal personal and political freedom. Parents with children in nurseries can use the internet to log on to CCTV cameras that monitor the activities in the class-room, though there have been some high-profile cases recently of the footage being inadequately protected and available to anyone.

Stores such as supermarkets and bookshops often offer loyalty card schemes to their customers. The benefit to the customer is in the form of saving points for rewards: the more points you have, the larger the reward you can claim. The benefit to the store is that purchases can be tracked, allowing them to send individualized incentive vouchers to keep customers returning to the same store. For example, when a supermarket notices (through the information in their loyalty card database of purchases) that the customer has started to purchase baby products, they may send out discount coupons for related items. Their hope is that by offering a 50p reduction on a £5 item, the customer will purchase the rest of their weekly shop at the same time, thus generating additional income for the store.

In a similar way to the supermarket schemes, digital television systems can track the programmes that you watch, 'remind' you when your favourite programmes begin and offer suitable viewing choices based on your programme history. Even basic systems offer the function of linking every episode of the series and automatically switching to the programme on the appropriate day and time.

Current trends

Multi-function devices (MFDs)

Over the years there has been a trend (resulting from consumer pressure and cost reduction) for devices, technologies and applications to become increasingly multi-functional; for example, printers are frequently replaced by printer/scanner/**fax**/copier machines and personal stereos by MP3 players offering additional functions such as video playback, photo display, radio reception and a clock, many of which can synchronize with your computer's organizer to import contacts, calendar and task lists.

Similarly, cash machines on the high street provide more than simple cash dispensing services. Users can check their balances, change the personal identification number on their card, pay cheques in, make charitable donations, withdraw foreign currency, pay bills, order statements and purchase mobile phone top-ups. In the latter case (for example) money is taken from the bank account and the customer types in their mobile phone number. A code is transmitted back to the mobile phone service provider, which credits the mobile phone accordingly.

It has become common to expect that many of our technological appliances should have more than one function and we are impressed by the range of functions available even though we may not know how to use the majority of them. One of the hidden perils of having an MFD is that when a device fails or is lost, several functions and sets of data can be lost instead of just one (for example, when a phone fails or is lost, the address book, telephone book, text message history, photographs and calendar entries are lost too). Until this happens most people do not even think about how to back up their data and many do not have the skills to do so, even should they wish to.

Reflection 2.2

List some of the convergent technologies that are available on the high street today. What are they used for, and can you identify any new trends?

Mobile telephones are no longer just telephones (and no longer have the physical attributes of a brick as they did in the 1980s); nowadays every mobile phone has a text message facility, and most can send pictures too. Very few mobile phones come without a still or video camera, the pictures from which can be uploaded (transferred by means of a cable or wireless connection) to a computer. Having this facility on a commonplace, everyday device means that most people are carrying a camera with them most of the time so important events can be captured more easily (for example, there is an increased likelihood of photographic evidence being captured at or around the scene of a crime or accident). Even basic models of mobile phone include an alarm function, a clock, a calculator and an answerphone function, and the more sophisticated models come complete with built-in satellite navigation units, **e-mail/** internet capabilities, video viewing software, games, a full address book system, programs that link up with computer software for typing/editing documents, and transferable memory cards that can swap between mobiles, cameras and MP3 players, for example.

Most of the newer, more sophisticated mobile phones offering extended features run a simplified version of the Microsoft **Windows** operating system, making application reuse very easy. This reduces the need for additional learning and makes use of existing knowledge of the operating system and applications since most people are already familiar with the Microsoft Windows environment. Internet-enabled phones such as the **BlackBerry, iPhone** and mobile digital assistants, combine the functionality of PDAs (such as **Palm Pilots** and **Psions**), which were popular in the 1990s, with mobile phone technology and traditional PC applications (such as web browsers, word processors, e-mail clients, spreadsheets and calendars). One of the main enablers for new phone-based applications has been affordable, unmetered internet access, in addition to a good web browser, which combine to allow for real-time data-fed applications, remote connectivity, access to web applications (the main processing being done remotely), secure access (**HTTPS**, Secure Socket Layer), access to search engines, and travel news.

Reflection 2.3

What features does your mobile phone have? Which ones do you use regularly? Are there features you do not know how to use?

E-books

Many mobile devices can also function as e-book readers whereby complete books can be stored, browsed and read on the devices without the need to print a hard copy. Whilst casual viewing on a mobile phone is useful, for more prolonged reading many people use devices with larger screens which can hold hundreds of books in memory, and a new revolution in e-books is slowly taking place. Modern versions of these e-book readers (such as Sony Reader, Amazon Kindle, **jetBook** and **BeBook**) use lower-power screen technologies, resulting in very long battery life (for example, a battery life of 7,000 page turns, equivalent to reading *War and Peace* five times over). This means that a school or university student could have all of their textbooks in one slim, lightweight, portable volume (removable media can be used to extend the amount of storage available on most e-books) and software supporting variable print size helps widen access to a greater audience. Future e-books may allow for moving graphics and sound to be used as part of a document, allowing multimedia clips to become part of a textbook, perhaps *showing* how to perform a task, rather than merely describing it. Smart use of current technology would allow for dictation software to read the book to the user.

Whilst the initial expense for the device is quite high, the e-books themselves will be much cheaper than printed versions and offer ecological advantages with a reduction in the use of paper and smaller manufacturing costs to the environment, whilst providing features not available in a printed copy, such as electronic searching. There are disadvantages with e-books too – as electronic devices they need charging (you have to remember to do this occasionally) and are susceptible to physical damage. However, most people are now very familiar with the care of electronic devices such as mobile phones, MP3 players, calculators and cameras.

Dynamic web content

Web pages used to be restricted to static, encyclopaedic pages, whereas nowadays we have coloured text, images, animations, sound and video and, most importantly, the data presented using these features is tailored to users' queries, preferences, locations and contexts. Sites from large companies such as the British Broadcasting Corporation (**BBC**) make good use of these features, with pages often containing hyperlinks to other parts of the same site (or to sites provided by other companies). It is very easy to become distracted when using the internet, and a session which began with a gardening query can quickly lead to cookery and history as we hop from link to link.

The next generation of websites are making use of 'mash-ups', which involve taking data from a variety of sources and presenting it all together. A simple example of this is when a shop's website contains a location map; they have usually not created their own, but brought over the relevant section from, say, Google Maps.

E-shopping

Internet shopping has become a practical alternative to mainstream purchasing of goods and services, not only for the housebound and those living in more rural areas, but also for those working long hours and those in search of lower prices. This has only recently become effective now that most shops have an online presence and their combined product range is enormous. Prices online are usually more competitive than in the high street due to lower overheads of retail space and staffing. One way that the high street stores have fought to retain business is by introducing 'reserve and collect' systems. This gives customers the 'online' price but with the option of collecting in person and avoiding the carriage costs and delays of using an online vendor.

In the internet shopping sector, we have seen tremendous growth in the number of buyers, but, more importantly, the web pages of these virtual shops carry more information and detail than ever before. Amazon is the UK's largest internet-based vendor of books, CDs and DVDs and offers the facility on many of their products to look at the item from different angles, listen to samples of audio and even read a few pages of books you may be interested in purchasing.

Without the boon of internet shopping, we would not have **eBay, uBid, Yahoo! Auctions, Freecycle** and many more. These sites have proved to be a useful way of selling (or simply passing on, in the case of Freecycle) second-hand (and obscure) goods to a wider audience than local newspapers can offer. This new way of buying and selling worked well on trust for a while, but once the trust was abused, individuals trading in this way needed a safer way to pay for goods and to receive payments. This led to a new section of the industry, where a company will act as a holding agent for transactions (for a small fee) and process credit card payments for individuals who would otherwise not be able to accept such a payment, one of the forerunners being **PayPal**. Some companies, such as **Interflora**, are now starting to use PayPal as an alternative to credit cards, which gives consumers more options when purchasing.

Reflection 2.4

Have you ever used a site such as eBay? Did your transaction go through smoothly? How did you pay for your purchases and how did you receive payment for goods sold? What advantages and disadvantages can you foresee in using a company such as PayPal? eBay carry expensive items such as cars for sale: what is the most expensive item you would consider buying in this way?

Social networking and leisure

With the decreasing price of computers and, more importantly, widely available, low-cost internet access coupled with data services to mobile phones, people are rapidly expanding their use of social networking technologies. With increasing bandwidth this has rapidly moved beyond simple text and voice conversations to video sharing and video conversations.

People should, however, be careful. Posting every action and decision one takes on a public internet site can be both foolish and harmful. If a stranger approached you in the street, it is unlikely that you would tell them your date of birth or where you live (or your maiden name, if you have one). In publishing such information online where people feel secure within their own environment the security risks that this poses have been ignored (refer to Chapter 1 for discussion on security issues). Compounding this problem are the people who publish on their page that they are about to go on holiday – this can surely only be inviting trouble? People would not write their life history day by day and stick it to the side of their house for all to view, but many seem happy to do this online. Adolescent pranks come back to haunt people in later life; employers can trace scandalous rumours and take legal action; and prospective employers can trawl such sites to get more personal information than one might like.

The BBC has reported several cases of workers losing their jobs through Facebook-related incidents. These have included a sacked 16-year-old office worker from Essex (BBC 2009a) who made disparaging remarks about her job on her Facebook page, and a Swiss worker (BBC 2009b) who had claimed to be too ill to work but was discovered using Facebook at home later the same day.

Reflection 2.5

Discuss the mistakes made by both employer and employee. How would you deal with such a situation if you were (i) the employee and (ii) the employer? If you have joined one of these sites, do you know how the privacy rules work or how to change the privacy settings? Does this affect your view of the usage of these sites? What do you use the site for?

Reflection 2.6

Carry out research to find these and other instances where a social networking site has led to a loss of employment. There are now self-help books available that explain all of the available features on these different social networking sites, such as social network gaming.

Similarly, the increased bandwidth is leading to a growth in on-demand entertainment, including BBC **iPlayer, Sky Player, Channel 4oD** and downloadable music. Indeed, these sites have become so popular that many mobile phones are supplied with the software necessary to access them preloaded in order to encourage users to access them from their phones throughout the day.

Business, e-communication and e-finance

Businesses are able to communicate with one another much more quickly using e-mail than by using standard mail sent through the post. Transactions which may have taken days to complete can now be finalized in minutes. There is no need for a company to wait for a cheque to arrive in the post, be deposited at the bank and then clear; if the customer uses a credit card to pay for the goods online, payment can be confirmed immediately. Most companies offer a next-day delivery service (for a premium fee) which can take the total transaction time (from ordering to delivery) down to hours rather than days. This can be hugely beneficial to the customer. It also allows businesses to run with much lower stocks of consumables, promoting a just-in-time principle where shop stock can be ordered daily if necessary and only when the stock reaches a certain level. With replenishments from suppliers being delivered sometimes on the day of ordering, businesses can keep stock levels low. This leads to better cash flow for the business without the fear of running out of stock. However, the picture is not all rosy as, unfortunately, e-commerce is susceptible to the same fraudulent practices outlined in Chapter 1.

Online banking is replacing telephone banking (popular in the 1990s), and customers use unique log-on passwords to allow them to set up their standing orders, make one-off payments, move money between accounts and pay bills without dealing directly with a member of the bank's personnel. This service is not constrained by time of day and there is no queuing involved. Online share trading can be done easily from home, allowing a new generation of people to dabble in the share market with comparative ease. Other examples of everyday e-commerce include insurance, television licencing, vehicle tax and utility bills.

E-green issues

Energy and recycling

In recent years both the general public and commercial businesses have been made increasingly aware of the cost (both financial and ecological) of running IT equipment, and there is substantial and rapidly growing pressure to reduce the energy consumption of IT equipment. Carr (2006) claimed that the yearly amount of electricity consumed by a Second Life **avatar** (a character in an online life simulation game) was the same as the average person living in Brazil. With the world deploying more and more IT equipment and with increasing energy prices and growing concern for environmental impact, 'green IT' and its initiatives are set to grow significantly in the forthcoming decade and beyond.

As individuals, we can help to lessen the impact of modern technology on the environment by buying energy-friendly products and by recycling our IT waste. Energy-friendly IT with the 'Energy Star' logo attached (visit the energystar.gov website for further information) will assure you that the product meets energy-efficiency regulations. When disposing of computer equipment, consider donating it to charities such as Computer Aid (visit the computeraid.org website for further information) which will relocate the machinery, or at the very least, dispose of it responsibly at a local recycling site.

Reflection 2.7

How do you think IT can help reduce your carbon footprint? What steps have you taken to reduce energy consumption of IT equipment in your home? How did you last dispose of unwanted IT equipment? Could you have put it to better use by donating it to a charity? Does your local council have a recycling scheme for IT equipment?

Changes in employment patterns

'Fashion comes full circle given time' we are told by the people in old photographs wearing clothes and haircuts that we are amused by. The same is true of many things and is starting to become true in the way we work. In the eighteenth century, most people lived in small villages and were self-sufficient, providing everything they needed from amongst themselves. There was a village blacksmith, a farrier, a weaver, a seamstress, and others would grow crops and rear livestock. The nineteenth century saw the Industrial Revolution, which took industries such as the textile industry into mass production in large mills and factories, and communities began to form around the mills in order for people to get work. The mill owner often paid part of their employees' wages in tokens which could only be spent in the shops and inns which he owned, further restricting movement between villages, and people could not easily relocate or change employers. This started to change with the decline of traditional industries, and, with the increase in commercial trade based in large towns and cities, people relocated into these in pursuit of work.

Reflection 2.8

Which professions allow opportunities for employees to work from home? What equipment would be needed? Have you ever worked from home? What are the advantages and disadvantages of working from home?

Among the disadvantages you may have discussed would be that if an employee does not have a separate workspace in the home, it can feel like they never leave work. By the very nature of working from home, there is less face-to-face interaction with other people, so staffroom banter and the associated rapport is lost. Without the build-up of such camaraderie, colleagues can be less willing to help out in times of crisis, as people often only go the extra mile in order to help someone they like. Some personalities find it very difficult to switch off from work, and their home and work lives suffer as a result.

With recent advances in technology, our working patterns are changing and people can once again work from home in an increasing number of professions. Office staff can type documents from home and collate presentations, teachers can prepare lessons, accountants can be based solely from home, and call centres can divert customers' calls to employees' homes during their working day. This has widened participation in the job market, opening it up more to returning workers and disabled people.

Case Study 2.1

Frances works for 'Four Winds', a small travel agency on the high street. When she started working there in the 1980s the job entailed answering queries by telephone, sending out invoices and assisting customers by use of holiday brochures to choose accommodation and flights (as well as being the human interface between the customer and large holiday companies).

Although the company has grown, they have a smaller presence on the high street now. The company manager has taken smaller premises for the travel agency but employs more people who work from their own homes. In accordance with the shift rota, the manager diverts calls to each employee's home telephone and they each have a company laptop with all of the necessary programs and databases preloaded. The laptops are linked to the internet, allowing company representatives to establish prices and confirm the details and bookings whilst the customer is on the line.

This use of new communication technologies appears to benefit everybody involved: the employee is no longer having to travel to the shop, consequently the manager has been able to take smaller and cheaper premises and some of those savings are being passed on to their customers.

Reflection 2.9

Is there anyone you know currently working from home either part-time or full-time? Would this still be possible without reliance upon IT systems?

Changes in working practices

Companies across the world can now hold meetings by telephone with participants in many different countries (in some cases with video links). Holding a meeting in this way greatly reduces the need to travel, saving the company a significant amount of money and time as well as being a more environmentally friendly option. In extreme cases, where jobs have highly specialized employment requirements or where candidates in the same country cannot be found (or where the requirements are more consultative in nature), employees may live in different countries than their employers and work remotely on a permanent basis.

Use of this type of technology is not limited to the business world; using instant chat programs, people across the world can 'chat' via the computer by typing, talking or holding video conversations (using a webcam). Whilst the picture and sound quality is not always as high as might be desired, it can be a very effective way to stay in touch with people who are far away.

When participating in a teleconference or an online text meeting, there is no scope for picking up on body language or facial expressions, and it can be easy to misinterpret a humorous comment as being a serious slur or offensive remark. It is worth remembering that when participants in the meeting are in different countries, they belong to different cultures and bring significantly different senses of humour and sensitivities to the table. Although we may feel that we are part of a virtual community, an inoffensive slang term in one country can be perceived as the height of rudeness in another country. It is not easy to understand every country's cultural nuances and it could be very easy to offend one's co-workers. This phenomenon has been repeatedly demonstrated in the commercial world where names of products do not translate well into other languages. A good example of this was when Rolls-Royce exported their Silver Mist to Germany without renaming it, apparently unaware that in German the word *Mist* means 'manure'.

For teleconferencing and for cheaper calls (especially internationally) many people are using VoIP. VoIP applications typically use a computer microphone and speaker to record in real time what is being said and to send it to a third party whilst simultaneously playing the sounds sent to them. In this way, if two computers are both connected to the internet (perhaps in different countries), what is said to one computer can be heard on the other and vice versa. This has been extended considerably by companies such as **Skype** to provide high-quality conference calls, VoIP breakout (whereby the Skype company can route your VoIP call to the nearest Skype centre and place a traditional call from there, allowing Skype calls to people not on a computer), call waiting and answerphone services. Wireless headsets incorporating headphones and a microphone or VoIP telephone handsets make using VoIP as easy as using a traditional telephone but at a much reduced cost.

Case Study 2.2

John trained as a museums officer; his job required him to be in the museum to deal with administration and visitors. Unfortunately, John suffered severe injuries following a car crash which left him unable to walk. Following the completion of his medical treatment he was unable to walk far enough or sit comfortably for long enough for the job to be viable.

During his rehabilitation, John gave consideration to starting his own business from home. His partner's hobby was cross-stitch, and it seemed as though it could be an easy business to set up at home.

John approached one of the major cross-stitch companies to enquire about starter packs for new retailers. A website was designed by a friend and soon John registered the business with the credit card companies. Since he was working from his own home, the only outlay was for the starter pack and the packaging in which to dispatch the goods that were sold. John paid for an advert in the back of a cross-stitch magazine advertising the new business and, although the business took off slowly, it grew steadily.

Reflection 2.10

What IT skills and equipment would John need in order to set up his new enterprise? Have you ever thought about setting up a business from home? Do you have the skills and equipment in order to do this?

Green futures

Virtualization

One of the business initiatives that has emerged in the past five years is **virtualization**, such as **VmWare**, whereby groups of several servers can be replaced with a single larger server, which behaves as though it is several 'virtual' servers. This has a whole host of benefits, for example:

- It saves space.
- It saves energy (both for servers and for air conditioning).
- It exploits the fact that most servers are relatively idle for most of the time.
- It allows for sharing of components, for example hard drives, network interfaces, memory, processors and so on.

Using virtualization technologies with redundant or load-balanced high-availability clustering allows businesses to reduce their server overhead significantly whilst providing fault tolerance and effective **back-up**.

Software licensing

Traditionally software was licensed on individual machines. For example, if an accountancy firm had 20 PCs it would need to purchase 20 individual copies of the accounting or spreadsheet software. As software has become more expensive and companies are trying to reduce costs, software usage more akin to rental has emerged. This is often known as 'software as a service' (**SAAS**): users of software are charged according to how much use they make of it. From the vendors' point of view this removes one of the largest obstacles to sale, initial outlay, and from the purchasers' point of view it makes trial use of new software much easier to justify financially. Common SAAS applications are Salesforce, **Gmail**, Google Reader, and Google Docs.

Hardware provision

In the same way that software is moving slowly towards SAAS, the same is happening to hardware (for large-scale computation and high-availability provision of web services), with 'hardware as a service' (**HAAS**) and 'cloud computing' (large distributed networks of processing capability and storage used and paid for by many different organizations). Clearly there are a host of issues to be overcome such as security, accounting, quality of service and availability, but the economic drivers (cost reductions of using shared resources) are resulting in significant growth in these areas, including Google Ads, Amazon Flexible Payments Service, PayPal, Open ID and Google Maps.

Summary of Key Points

- IT is here to stay and is growing in popularity.
- Internet shopping has huge advantages, but they need to be measured against the security risks and potential loss of some high street stores.
- We all need to be more aware of the green issues surrounding our use of IT and alter our behaviour accordingly.
- The increased use of IT has allowed our societies to alter the structure of their working patterns.

Further reading

Abram, C. and Pearlman, L. (2008) *Facebook for Dummies*. Indianapolis: Wiley.

Fitton, L., Gruen, M. and Poston, L. (2009) *Twitter for Dummies*. Indianapolis: Wiley.

Miller, M. (2008) *Cloud Computing: Web-Based Applications that Change the Way You Work and Collaborate Online*. Indianapolis: Que.

Ryan, D. and Jones, C. (2009) *Understanding Digital Marketing: Marketing Strategies for Engaging the Digital Generation*. London: Kogan Page.

Warschauer, M. (1999) *Electronic Literacies: Language, Culture and Power in Online Education*. Mahwah, NJ: Lawrence Erlbaum Associates.

3

Aspects of teaching and learning IT

In this chapter we will focus on:

- Inherent challenges of teaching generic IT in specialist industries.
- Making the learning as real as possible.
- The challenges of teaching in a rapidly changing subject.
- Keeping up to date with CPD initiatives.

The rapid developments in both convergent and emerging technologies (see Chapter 2), the increasing miniaturization of 'go anywhere' devices and the developing green agendas all impact extensively on the teaching of IT. Some teachers may liken the uncertainty of having to keep up with such change as feeling like having to step into a black hole, not quite knowing what is in store and what will become of their knowledge which is constantly being updated and simultaneously outmoded. IT can be exciting, invigorating and perhaps at times a little scary as we try to keep up to date with our students, peers, employers' needs and changes in technology. This is what makes CPD so important.

It is the responsibility of every professional teacher to keep up to date with new teaching methods and developments in their subject. CPD is essential for all teachers to keep abreast of new qualifications, ideas and pedagogies. It is especially important that IT teachers keep up to date to ensure that their students are as well equipped as possible for the real world of work in which IT features so heavily and evolves so quickly.

Many job descriptions nowadays ask for candidates who are 'computer literate'. One problem that faces many job seekers is knowing exactly what being 'computer literate' means: how much knowledge is required and which applications should they be able to use? Each employer will have their own idea of what 'computer literacy' is. This is discussed further in Chapter 4, but it is generally accepted by society that a computer-literate person should be able to use a word processor, e-mail software, search the internet with proficiency and not be too alarmed when asked to use what may at first appear to be an entirely new program. Transferable skills are paramount in teaching and learning IT. Anyone who holds a qualification such as the European Computer Driving Licence (**ECDL**), discussed further in Chapter 5, will have learned to use a range of programs and can reasonably claim to have computer literacy sufficient for the workplace.

Due to the transient nature of IT, the definition of 'computer literacy' will change over time and, as teachers, we must adapt our lessons and projects to the demands of newer generations of technologies and applications as and when they arrive. As we have seen in Chapter 2, much IT is now multi-functional and each new package we learn is likely to have a positive impact in other areas, such as the downloading of music files to a computer.

Reflection 3.1

What do you consider to be necessary achievements in order for a job applicant to state that they have a high level of computer literacy? How well equipped do your learners feel they need to be? Do they meet these criteria yet?

Challenges with highly specialized IT

Many fields of employment are so specialized in nature that the software applications that employees use are virtually unique and will only be encountered or taught within their particular field. For example, there are no generally available applications for controlling and analysing the results from MRI scanners used in medicine, or for controlling the mixing of pigments in a paint or cosmetics factory. In such specialized fields, employers cannot expect training institutions to provide courses in these applications (unless they specifically fund such courses for their employees), and instead have to rely on options such as the following:

- Attempting to recruit staff from other organizations in their field ('head-hunting') – although this tends to only apply to high-calibre staff on large salaries, such as consultants.
- Employing specialist contractors in the field – such contractors typically move from company to company on short-term contracts and are usually very highly paid. In some cases this is advantageous as the company avoids incurring costs associated with recruitment and induction inherent with permanent staffing.
- Employing staff with recognized computer literacy skills together with experience in similar or related applications and then adding to those skills by in-house training or utilization of specially funded courses provided by software companies or quality third-party organizations.

Case Study 3.1

Sunita wanted to train as a legal secretary. Having checked on the internet, she found that she only needed to add general secretarial and computer-literacy skills to her five

GCSEs before applying for her first post in the sector. She completed the ECDL qualification and was successful in her application.

During the next five years Sunita found her computer-literacy skills useful but additionally had to learn how to use specific courtroom and police software applications in order to process legal cases. She learnt the new IT applications from more experienced staff members employed by the company.

Several years later Sunita was offered an opportunity to advance her career into paralegal work. Although she felt ready for the challenge, when she started the job, she found that the IT systems used were different from those she had used as a legal secretary. This worried her because, despite her previous training and work experience at the same company, she continually had to ask colleagues for help.

Reflection 3.2

How do you think Sunita could have better prepared herself for her change of position? What could the paralegal department have done during Sunita's induction period?

There should have been no reason for Sunita to feel inadequate or unprepared for her new job. With many companies nowadays, computer literacy is as specific a skill as can be asked for, as many have their own in-house systems which people will not encounter elsewhere. Such systems are so specific to the job that it is not profitable to release the software to the general public. General computer literacy is a useful start when learning to use new software as many of the features are generic and therefore common to most packages. Therefore, the skills that we acquire when learning to use a software package are often transferable. For example, most systems would have the capability to open a file, save and print, though the shortcut keys and menu selections may be different. This is why it is vital that when we teach IT we teach not only mechanical skills, but also how to reason and analyse. In this way cognition becomes an embedded part of the learning process and as important as the end product.

Case Study 3.2

Dean works in a library in the South of England but is moving to the North of Scotland. He applies for a position in a library near his new residence and is granted an interview. During the interview, he is questioned about his computer skills. He proceeds to outline how he would carry out various tasks on the computer system in the library in order to demonstrate his knowledge. When his interviewers look blank during his explanation, he describes some more complex procedures in the hope that this will be what they were looking for. Fortunately, one interviewer spots that the confusion has started because the library which Dean previously worked for was using a different system than the one used in Scotland. Since Dean's IT skills were transferable (the processes were the same, even though the specific menu combinations varied) he was given the job.

Reflection 3.3

What skills do you think Dean will bring to the job that someone without a background in library work would not? Can you think of other professions where the computer systems may vary between similar companies?

Company-specific versus generic software applications

When a company is looking to acquire a software package (either for the first time or to replace legacy software), they typically produce as comprehensive a list of requirements of the software as they can. Once this list is complete, the evaluation of candidate software packages begins and the most appropriate package is procured, with consideration being given to software, hardware and training. In larger establishments, the services of a business analyst may be used for this purpose. For small organizations this tends to be 'off-the-shelf' software which is written to appeal to as large a number of customers in as large a number of professions as possible (to maximize the software company's profits). Such software probably covers their needs to a large extent but is unlikely to be a perfect fit. For larger organizations with larger budgets, if the facilities provided by the generic, commonly available applications do not cover enough of their requirements, they may approach software vendors to enquire as to the costs of extending existing products or writing new ones specifically for their needs. The situation is very similar to buying a suit; one can either go for an off-the-peg suit which will fit most people fairly well for a moderate price, or if one has a large enough budget and is not willing to accept a 'tolerable fit' then one can have a custom-made suit which will be a much better fit, but (inevitably) significantly more expensive.

The difference between highly specialized fields, such as MRI scanning and paint manufacture, and more generalized employment, such as clerical, financial and stock control, is that the former tend to have custom applications (as there are no generally available applications) but the latter can probably find off-the-shelf applications fitting their needs reasonably well and only the largest organization will consider procuring bespoke applications.

As with highly specialized IT, organizations that opt for customized applications (rather than working with and around off-the-shelf applications) need to consider additional factors such as software maintenance costs, which are much higher with bespoke applications, the inability to recruit staff with appropriate experience and additional training costs.

Designing projects to mirror industry

While it is clearly highly desirable to teach students as much as possible that is going to be relevant to their real-world use of computers, teachers need to be careful (especially for examined qualifications) to ensure that they cover the entire syllabus and in sufficient depth that their students obtain a firm grasp of the basics.

Similarly, when designing projects for students to undertake, it is good practice to try to replicate the kinds of activities that they will be doing when they start work, but teachers need to be careful not to make their projects too specific to a given profession; or, if the projects are specific to a given profession, that a range of projects is undertaken, or available to cover a range of different scenarios, for example a project aimed at secretarial use of computers (word processing), another aimed at financial use of computers (spreadsheets), another aimed at publishing (desktop publishing), another at web design. Specific experience working with specialized IT systems is most appropriately learned through apprenticeships and work experience, and these are discussed further in Chapter 4.

The projects that we set for our students need to be realistic. As most of us learn from our experiences, after all, if we feel that we have achieved something useful, we are more likely to be able to reproduce it in a similar situation. It is a good idea to establish links with local community groups and businesses and to liaise with them when designing coursework scenarios. It may turn out that one of your students designed the entire system that the local scout leader uses for his administration purposes. When students of all ages can see that their endeavours are worthwhile, they feel a greater sense of purpose throughout the project. If a group of students can design an office system to meet customer specifications, they will be more confident when trying out new areas of the software packages to see what other features might be needed in a different suite of specifications.

Case Study 3.3

Suki has been following an IT course at school. They have covered the basics of word processing, spreadsheets and databases independently and have just moved on to working with multiple packages together. The example that they used in class was to set up a database of their relatives in order to create mailing labels for Christmas cards. Suki designed her database and was pleased with the results when she merged it into labels using the word-processing software. Suki had a weekend job at a beauty parlour, greeting clients and answering the telephone. She was asked to write out envelopes for advertising leaflets to be posted. As she sat writing them, she thought how much easier it would be if the database of clients were computerized instead of being held in a card index system. She approached the manager with the idea of offering to do it for her and was paid during the school holidays to computerize the system ready for use in mailshots and to ensure that computer information is kept according to the requirements of the Data Protection Act (1988).

Reflection 3.4

List the projects that you set your students. Analyse whether they are outdated or are transferable to different scenarios. Could you approach local community projects to access their input into useful and meaningful projects?

Time lag

Due to the rapid evolution of software, it is very easy to get left behind with new features in applications as the costs and logistics of keeping up to date are prohibitive. This phenomenon creates a time delay between what a student or teacher may be using at home or at an academic institution and in the workplace. Many people still use legacy software. Take, for example, operating systems such as Microsoft Windows XP, which is still widely in use, especially in the home. Large business and academic institutions may have only just completed rolling out Microsoft Vista as the update to this, knowing that Microsoft Windows 7 has already been released and is preinstalled on the majority of new computers.

With the updated operating systems come newer versions of existing software packages and new-to-market products. Most proficient users may have a short period of readjustment when they start to use these new packages, but the manufacturers design the software so that skills are easily transferable between packages. Backward compatibility of software is often built in so that newer applications can still open documents created in previous versions, though frustration can occur when a student is working across multiple platforms as files created in the new versions cannot be accessed on computers with older software versions, unless the user remembers to save a file as an older file type. In our experience, this can cause issues when newer students have up-to-date versions of software and the establishment at which they are learning at has an older version.

At some stage, though, as software support diminishes and compatibility issues increase, upward migration will be needed. If updates have not been regularly undertaken the costs not only of purchasing software licences, but also of retraining will be significant. Migration is usually prompted by one or more of a number of causes:

- A compelling new feature (users need a feature in a new release that is not available in an older release and are forced to upgrade).

- Maintenance is withdrawn for the older release (most organizations have maintenance contracts in place to ensure that they can get support for their software should problems arise and to allow them to gain access to new features and bug-fixes released for their software). When maintenance is discontinued, most organizations take the opportunity to upgrade and/or re-evaluate which applications are needed in their workplace.

- Compatibility with third parties such as suppliers or partner organizations must be taken into account. Whilst backward compatibility from new versions of software to older versions is common, forward compatibility is rarely possible. So, when a new version of an application is released and used by a subset of people within (or outside) an organization, users of the older version can no longer open their files and are forced to upgrade.

However, an interesting twist in the rapid evolution of computer applications and the race to acquire current skills was highlighted by the so-called 'millennium bug'.

Many older programs had been written with two-digit year coding so that at the millennium a year entered as 00 would default to 1900. The need for staff with experience in legacy languages and applications such as Fortran and Cobol, which had not been taught for many years, to recode the legacy applications, especially in financial and database applications, was colossal. Worried organizations paid excessively high salaries to programmers with experience in these languages to fix the applications and to be available should their applications fail.

Reflection 3.5

How much would it cost to replace all the hardware and software in your establishment? Which local firms could you approach to request sponsorship or donations? What would be the advantages and disadvantages of involving local businesses in your establishment?

Interestingly, students can complete their studies and enter the workplace with application experience either ahead or behind that of their employer's applications as can be seen in the following two case studies:

Case Study 3.4

In some cases, taught courses can take two or more years to complete and cover a large number of applications. By the time an employee begins working, the applications they have studied may already have been superseded and they may be unfamiliar with new applications that have been released while they were studying. This is especially true if the employer's requirements dictate a very recent version of the software, such as a compelling new feature, maintenance withdrawal or compatibility issues, whereas the training organization can happily work with older (cheaper) versions of the software running on older (cheaper) hardware and does not need all of the newest features. Ideally training organizations should aim to provide the most up-to-date software they can, budgets permitting.

Case Study 3.5

Often large organizations are reluctant to adopt the latest versions of software (due to potential instability of the newest versions of operating systems and applications, the costs of adopting new releases including software, hardware, training) and they continue to use their existing software until a compelling event occurs (as described previously), or until their requirements change. In this manner, many organizations are running relatively old software which may lag behind that which their new employees have been taught. This does not necessarily cause any problems (other than employee frustration at missing the newer features) and may well be advantageous from the employer's point of view as they already have staff trained in the new releases who should only need a refresher course when they upgrade, rather than a full training course showing all of the new features.

Employees can also start with a current set of application skills but, after several years in a company where the applications are not upgraded and where training is not offered, those skills start to become dated and of less value than those offered by more recently trained employees. After many years their outdated skill set can make moving jobs difficult and seeking re-employment after redundancy challenging. This is why CPD is so important.

Continuing professional development

Unlike professions such as tailoring, decorating and carpentry for which styles, colours and patterns might change but the skills required to perform the jobs remain similar, in IT the very tools themselves (applications and operating systems) change frequently and rapidly. For this reason, for an IT sector worker to remain a desirable employee throughout his or her working life (probably in excess of 50 years), it is imperative that they keep their skills and experiences both up to date and spanning a broad spectrum. Recognition of this is central to notions of CPD whereby individuals identify what skills they have, what skills they will need in the future and the route by which they can move from the former to the latter. As the name suggests, it is a continual process as employees continue to chase and acquire the skills they need for their current and their future roles. The importance of CPD is increasingly recognized and plays a prominent part in professional bodies such as the British Computer Society (**BCS**).

Allied with the need to remain a desirable employee is the need to acquire a broad set of current skills to allow freedom to move within the job market (when or if necessary). Whereas jobs half a century ago were 'for life', nowadays they are often for five years or less and remaining appealing in such a fluid job market requires a large set of demonstrable, transferable skills.

This is often difficult to achieve in a company which uses old and stable applications and provides little (if any) training. It can also be difficult to achieve in small organizations which are only concerned with hiring employees with the skills they need to get them through the next year or two and do not necessarily care about developing their staff for the more distant future. This is especially true in challenging economic times where companies are fighting for survival from month to month and are not looking to their medium-term or long-term future needs.

Employees can study new technologies and use new applications outside working hours, but it can be time-consuming and expensive to acquire the necessary hardware, software, training and books. It should also be cautioned that unless a qualification can be obtained it might just be viewed by a potential new employer as a hobby and not a genuinely acquired usable skill. Person specifications or job adverts often ask for a number of years of experience using a particular application.

Reflection 3.6

Do you consider yourself to have the necessary digital life skills? Do you need to update any of your skills or acquire new ones? In what other ways can employers, IT teachers and potential employees in the IT industry update their skills?

One way for teachers to update their own CPD is to attend conferences or take part in online discussions focused either on teaching IT specifically or on more general associated issues such as assessment or new legislation. Examples of organizations that host such conferences are the Special Schools and Academies Trust, E-Skills UK, the National Institute of Adult Continuing Education (**NIACE**), Lifelong Learning UK (**LLUK**), the Lifelong Learning and Skills Improvement Service (**LSIS**) as well as various awarding bodies including Assessment and Qualifications Alliance (**AQA**), Oxford Cambridge and RSA Examinations (**OCR**) and EdExcel.

A further very enjoyable way of updating your knowledge of emerging trends in technology is to attend a technology trade fair. The UK's best-known educational exhibition is the British Educational Training and Technology (**BETT**) show. This is held in London each year, usually at Olympia in January, and is free for all teachers and educators. Technology companies from around the world vie to demonstrate their latest educational hardware, software, peripherals and training portfolios. Teachers can try out the products and see for themselves whether they will help to motivate students or ease the task of reporting to parents or assessment bodies. The range of products is enormous and demonstrates how huge an industry education technology has become.

Reflection 3.7

Research online when the next BETT show is taking place. Even if you are unable to attend, there is usually an abundance of ideas on a wide range of topics listed.

For employees seeking to gain additional training, or training unrelated to their current job, for example to diversify their skills and therefore increase their employment prospects, non-work-based training might be the solution. With the ability to provide high-quality, interactive, multimedia presentations across the internet, there are now many companies providing web-based training that can be undertaken at work or at home. This can be done over a flexible time period to fit in with a person's lifestyle. These online courses are usually well structured and present the course material in clear, readily accessible modules, each of which is usually followed by a test or examination. These courses are often accompanied by printed notes and exercises that are mailed to the student. There is often either an online student group (where questions can be asked and problems discussed) or an assigned online tutor (with e-mail and telephone access) or both. Some of these courses have an examination at the end which is either taken online or in traditional 'examination hall' style settings. For example, **Cisco** Computer Certified Network Associate (**CCNA**), Cisco Certified

Network Professional (**CCNP**) and Cisco Certified Internetwork Expert (**CCIE**) qualifications can all be studied for online and the candidate only needs to attend the final examination at an approved venue (to ensure that appropriate examination conditions can be enforced).

Whilst students can obtain experience and qualifications online, or through more traditional courses, employers are still wary of employing staff with the appropriate qualifications but no experience – after all, who would volunteer to be a brain surgeon's first patient or a car mechanic's first customer?

Another benefit of online learning is that it can be provided for people where there are insufficient numbers of users in a particular location to make hosting a course viable. For example, if a local college wants to run a course in word processing, or host an ECDL course, it is likely to be well attended. If, however, a hospital wants to send its radiologists on a course in how to use the latest MRI imaging software to broaden their skills it can probably only afford online training for them (provided by the software manufacturer) rather than the alternative of paying to fly their staff to their software provider's premises (incurring prolonged staff absence, travel and subsistence costs and so on). These types of courses tend to lean more toward the provision of recorded training videos and presentations, seminars and interactive demonstrations rather than formal taught courses with examinations at the end.

This is to guard against the qualifications which they accredit becoming unrepresentative of the qualification holder's ability to perform competently using contemporary technologies and applications. Some training institutions place an expiry date on their qualifications. Other qualifications need refreshing or they 'expire' and the qualification holders are no longer allowed to claim to have the qualification – for example, most Cisco certifications expire within three years and have to be renewed or upgraded. Microsoft examinations typically do not expire but are tied to versions of the products, for example Microsoft Certified Systems Engineer (**MCSE**) 2000, Microsoft Certified Systems Administrator (**MCSA**) 2000, 2003, 2008. Whilst these expiring or 'ageing' qualifications are popular with employers, they are not popular with employees as most people like to be able to retain the qualifications they have earned. However, it does impose greater pressure on employers to provide training to keep their employees' qualifications current as candidates are unlikely to wish to join an organization in which their qualifications will atrophy.

For large complex applications and operating systems there are a large number of qualifications each aimed at a specific role – for example, MCSA, MCSE, Microsoft Certified Application Developer (**MCAD**), Microsoft Certified Solution Developer (**MCSD**) and Microsoft Certified Architect (**MCA**). In this way, if an employer hires an employee with a current qualification in the relevant field they can be sure that the employee will be proficient in that specific technology for that specific role.

With an increasing diversity of qualifications, including traditional GCSEs, **AS** levels, A levels, degrees, new IT qualifications, such as ECDL, Computer Literacy and Information Technology (**CLAiT**) and vendor-specific qualifications such as MCSE, CCNA and CCIE, it is becoming increasingly difficult for employers to assess the validity and level of a candidate employee's qualifications. There are also an increasing number of fraudulent companies (usually outside the UK) which 'sell' bogus qualifications or provide qualifications without sufficient course content.

This has led to many employers using qualifications only for crude screening of candidates (together with telephone interviews) and then relying on face-to-face interviews and in-house testing of the candidate's relevant experience together with prolonged probation periods during which an employee must demonstrate their worth.

Summary of Key Points

- Occupational currency via CPD for those involved in such a rapidly evolving sector is essential. For IT teachers, CPD is similarly vital to keep abreast of new ideas and to use interesting and exciting teaching strategies in their teaching.
- By being confident in new technology and some of the specialist technology you will be in the best position to help students find employment.
- Increasingly IT qualifications need to be combined with industry experience, and this is discussed further in Chapter 4.

4

Preparing for work in IT

In this chapter we will focus on:

- Functional skills and the purpose of digital literacy.
- The gender imbalance in the IT industry.
- Creating and sustaining partnerships for work experience and apprenticeships.

Purposes of digital literacy

The digital divide and the economic importance of digital skills were discussed in Chapter 2. Such digital skills at GCSE level equate to a set of functional skills in the use of a relatively small subset of IT applications and were positioned alongside literacy and numeracy as a basic skill in 2001 when the *Skills for Life* report stated:

> New technology is significantly increasing the need to read, write and use numbers confidently and effectively. Before long, those who cannot use a computer and access the internet may be as disadvantaged as those who are now unable to write or add up, and information technology skills will be as basic a skill as literacy and numeracy.
>
> (Department for Education and Employment (**DfEE**) 2001, p. 9)

The curriculum and assessment strategies at this level and within the national Skills for Life agenda are designed to equip the student with the necessary functional skills to enter the workplace or higher education with a nationally recognized level of IT literacy.

One of the most important basic skills needed for life and work today at this level is an ability to search the internet for specific information. However, the ability to find and extract information from the internet, as with any other source, is not the same as the ability to sift, summarize and make sense of information. These additional abilities are termed 'information literacies' and can be defined as the ability 'to recognize when information is needed and ... to locate, evaluate, and use effectively the needed information' (Beetham *et al.* 2009). They are perhaps some of the abilities that the executive chairman of Marks and Spencer, Sir Stuart Rose, famously coined as 'the 21st Century equivalent of metal bashing' (Jameson 2009).

According to Beetham *et al.* (2009) in the Literacy Learning for the Digital Age project, 'to date the focus has largely been on individual use in the context of a specific task or problem. The idea of information literacy may need to be extended to include sharing and collaboration, and to accommodate ethical dimensions.' As online library catalogues, electronic scanning of books and the use of e-readers gather pace, the necessity for students to be information literate in this way will also increase.

Currently an A* grade at GCSE does not necessarily guarantee that students are information literate or that they can combine information with their own knowledge to create and innovate. Castells (2000) argues the need for a broader definition to include this notion of innovation, advocating a need for the term 'digitally literate' which is not simply synonymous with the facility to locate information, but with the need to develop a forward-thinking society of individuals who use information to create new knowledge.

This might not be such an issue for debate if it were not for the falling numbers of students taking GCSE ICT courses or going on to A level (Department for Business, Enterprise and Regulatory Reform (BERR) 2009). The significant reduction in students taking IT as a subject will seriously undermine Britain's drive towards the high-skills, knowledge-based economy that the *Digital Britain* report (BIS 2009a) stresses.

Indeed, as the internet information base expands exponentially, proficiency in accessing information becomes the ability to filter information for relevance, currency and accuracy. Equipping learners with enough political, economic and social awareness to surf safely and discerningly requires the development of not only functional skills but also a degree of critical thinking skills. These are the skills that Prensky (2009) terms 'digital wisdom' and what Orr *et al.* (2001, p. 457) define as the 'ability to locate, manage, critically evaluate, and use information for problem solving, research, decision making, and continued professional development'.

However, the other side of this debate must also be recognized. While, on the one hand, in the name of widening participation and transparency, the internet has become the preferred channel of distributing information, on the other, paradoxically, it is also a means of further marginalizing those on the other side of the digital divide.

Those unable to access the internet, either because they do not have physical access or because they lack relevant skills, are also unable to access information on how to register children for school, school and college attendance records, to find information about access to adult learning and literacy courses, to complete online job applications and government benefit forms. As information becomes increasingly focused through a single communication channel of digitized media, digital literacy becomes vital for individuals in society.

Writers such as Norris (2001) and Van Dijk (2005) recognize that the lack of digital literacy and information literacy has a marginalizing effect. Without access to information it is becoming increasingly difficult for many to secure their democratic rights, and the so-called digital divide is manifested as an 'information divide'. The very drive for democracy that the government espouses is the means by which accessibility to the information is denied. Retrieval of national and local government information is routed through 'one-stop' websites in a bid to become more efficient and in the view of Norris (2001) represents a misguided attempt to improve access to information. Without access to information the criteria for informed civic participation in democratic process cannot be achieved.

> **Reflection 4.1**
>
> In your view, should IT be hailed as a way to produce the elusive 'knowledge economy' (Castells, 2000) that successive governments have sought since the 1980s? If so, why, and how can it be achieved? What role does it, and should it, have in widening participation in education, social engagement and democratic purposes?

The gender gap in IT

The use of IT is now commonplace in education, the home and the workplace. According to research by BERR (2009), 1.2 million people are employed in IT professional occupations and are responsible for 3 per cent of the total UK economy. However, they also identified that the male/female ratio is significantly skewed, with only 23 per cent of the IT workforce being female. This figure compares unfavourably with the proportion of females in the remainder of the UK national workforce, which is 45 per cent.

In 2008, figures from the Women in IT Scorecard (BERR 2009) indicated that the gender imbalance begins at GCSE level, with 12 per cent fewer females taking ICT, and becomes a more dramatic trend at A level, with females accounting for only 9 per cent of the candidates in Computing and 38 per cent in ICT. Table 4.1 demonstrates this trend in detail.

At higher education level, women interested in taking computer science degrees account for only 15 per cent of the total number of applications. These women are

Table 4.1   Percentages of females/males in UK education and the workplace in IT-related subjects, 2008

IT/ICT discipline	Female	Male
GCSE ICT	44	56
Diploma in IT	Figures not yet available	
A-level IT	9	91
A-level ICT	38	62
Computer science degree	15	85
Academic staff in IT	20	80
IT professional careers	19	81

Source: BERR (2009).

80 per cent more likely to be taught by male than by female academic staff, and if they enter the IT workforce they will be outnumbered by males 5 to 1. The report also indicates that most female professionals that do enter the industry are considerably more likely to be employed in less well-paid occupations such as database administration and IT support. The gender gap is not restricted to the UK, with the highest female representation in the IT workforce across Europe set at 30 per cent in Ireland and Italy.

Reflection 4.2

What are the male/female ratios in your establishment undertaking qualifications and on the teaching staff? Is there a difference between male/female student success rates? If so, how do you account for such differences?

The IT industry as a whole is highly competitive and formal qualification levels are highly respected and valued, with 60 per cent of those working in the IT industry holding a qualification at level 4 or higher, compared to 33 per cent for other industries (BERR 2009). When analysing these figures by gender, it becomes obvious that there will be considerably fewer opportunities for women to enter the profession unless they hold an IT qualification, and if only 15 per cent are studying for a degree this will have a serious impact on the gender imbalance. The highest professional qualification awarded by the BCS is Chartered IT Professional (**CITP**) status. In 2008 of the 19,000 men and women who took the examinations, only 8 per cent were female.

The gender imbalance is of great concern to employers, especially as females who do engage with IT consistently achieve higher grades than their male counterparts. The government and industry see women as an underutilized resource that could bring different perspectives, insight and innovation to the economy. According to BERR (2009, pp. 2–3), the 'gender divide stems in part from the ICT education system with negative experiences of GCSE ICT affecting future subject choices'. But what can be done?

Engaging women and girls in IT

As part of the research for this book, we informally interviewed girls who were taking ICT at GCSE or diploma level to determine what motivated them to choose to study the subject. One of the main reasons they gave was, perhaps unsurprisingly, whether they thought they would enjoy the subject or not based on their experiences of IT in previous years. They were also highly influenced by the thoughts and choices of their peers, parents and older siblings, and the future careers that they saw themselves choosing. Many stated that they were also motivated by social networking sites and what jobs they saw women doing in the media. When asked specifically about their GCSE course almost all the girls said they found it 'boring', and the reason for this they said was that they spent too much time printing out evidence, following demonstrations by the teacher and having to memorize various functions. They found little or no connection to their own interests or the real world. In the teacher-led demonstrations they said that everyone was held back to the pace of the slowest member of the group, while the teacher demonstrated something that quite often they had already done at home. Only one girl we spoke to said she would continue to A level and that was because she thought a career in IT would fit in around having a family, emulating her mother who worked from home.

Reflection 4.3

Undertake a small-scale research project. Ask some of your male and female learners what motivates them to learn IT. Now ask some learners who are not learning IT what deters them from doing so.

E-Skills UK (2009b) are very aware of the gender issue and have put considerable thought into producing courseware to make the learning more imaginative. The Computer Club for Girls (CC4G) was set up in 2005 in an attempt to redress the gender imbalance in the IT industry by inviting local, national and international employers to provide opportunities to meet some of the UK's female technology leaders. The meetings allow students to hear about potential careers, different organizations and how IT can be used to combine working from home with a career. Other opportunities include 'Bring a Girl to Work' initiatives, holiday clubs and the provision of teaching resources and courseware designed specifically to engage girls.

CC4G has recently widened its approach and has now designed innovative and interesting courseware and resources for both girls and boys undertaking IT subjects in schools mapped to the National Curriculum at Key Stages 2 and 3 for all students. This is in response to the 25 per cent overall reduction, from 116,030 in 2002 to 85,600 in 2008, in the number of students taking ICT at GCSE level, both male and female, that was highlighted in the BERR (2009) report.

For many women who did not or were unable to engage with IT qualifications at 16 or those who wish to change career and retrain in IT, the ECDL examinations awarded by the BCS and Businesses and Technology Council (**BTEC**) qualifications tend to dominate the sector. Second chances for women to engage in an IT career are provided by private training companies, adult education classes run by local authorities and other further education colleges. These and other qualifications are discussed in more detail in Chapter 5.

In adult and community education classes the gender balance swings the other way, and the vast majority of students learning IT are women. Some of these students are working with computers already and are hoping to 'prove' their ability in a highly competitive, largely qualifications-led industry. Others want to learn how to use IT in their everyday lives, and still others want to be able to engage with their children and grandchildren. Most of these classes allow the students to continue to work while studying part-time.

> **Reflection 4.4**
>
> How would you advise someone who wishes to retrain in IT to go about it? Do you know where courses are held locally?

Linking education to the workplace

The 14–19 Diploma in IT was designed as a flexible qualification which not only requires classroom-based approaches to learning, but also involves employers in its delivery. Employers have played an integral part in the creation of the Diploma in IT, which requires 50 per cent work-related learning. This requirement is a vital aspect of the qualification and means that students are provided with opportunities to discover how IT is used in the real business world and moves away from traditional routes that have focused exclusively on IT user skills that many of the girls interviewed earlier in this chapter described as 'boring'. There are also sandwich placements and apprenticeship schemes available, all designed to bring the real world of IT to life using real-life situations. This is not a new concept and it has been the dominant form of learning in some higher education subjects for a number of years. What is new is the broadening of such opportunuities to a wider age range.

It is as yet difficult to judge whether the Diploma in IT will be adopted universally, but other initiatives make it increasingly necessary for teachers and lecturers to become more familiar with local and national employers to help students find work experience placements and to connect students with IT apprenticeships where students can earn and learn at the same time. Partnerships with local authorities, local and national employers will be vital in securing valuable, up-to-date knowledge and skills for the IT workforce.

Work experience allows students to experience IT within a business environment, contextualizing the learning and providing a course that is likely to motivate and connect students directly with the workplace. Students who experience such authentic work-related activities can understand the relevance of classroom-based learning and relate technology to business and community more readily. The best programmes allow students on work placements to discover first-hand what it is like to approach challenges, handle projects, and innovate using their IT and personal skills.

Opportunities and challenges of work placements

The idea behind any work experience placement is to give students valuable experience and insights into what is involved in the real-world use of computers in a commercial environment. These placements vary in length and can range from a full-time placement for up to a year, as in sandwich degrees, to a couple of weeks or one day a week. The Education and Skills Act (2008) means that the participation age will rise to 17 from 2013 and 18 from 2015 and all young people will be expected to continue in some form of education or training. For many this will mean either continuing in school or moving to a college, studying full-time for GCSEs, A levels, foundation skills or the new Diploma in IT. Others will follow the newly expanded apprenticeship route which is currently being extended further. For those entering the job market part-time, education will also be part of their working week as they will be expected to gain further skills and qualifications at an educational establishment, such as attending college one day a week. These initiatives will reduce the number of young people classified by government as not in education, employment or training (NEET).

It will be the job of the local authorities to control funding for the 16–19 sector and allocations will be made in collaborative partnerships with educational establishments, careers guidance agencies, support organizations and employers to establish opportunities for young people through apprenticeships. They will also be required to support young people at risk through 'learning and support agreements'. The time line is very tight and the race is on to prepare and gear up over the next three years.

Options for 14–19-year-olds

The routes and options available for young people therefore are set to broaden, and change always has the potential to confuse. Chapter 5 describes the range of qualifications available to this age group in more detail.

Many of the new arrangements are very intricate and will require a great deal of forethought and planning to be successful for students, local authorities, educational establishments and employers. Each situation will vary according to, for example, the age of the student, where they will be placed and how much supervision they will require. The following list indicates some of the challenges posed by organizing work placements successfully:

- *Match organizations with student ability and interests.* Provide a short academic profile of each student for the employer, introducing their strengths. Be open about what challenges the student may face while in their placement, such as getting somewhere on time, organizing their work or being a self-starter.

- *Ensure that the student can get to and from the work placement safely.* Perhaps help students to research this for themselves and involve parents or guardians with the decision-making process.

- *Check that the organization is suitable.* Do you need to ensure that personnel in the employing agency have been vetted by the Criminal Records Bureau? Are they on the local authority 'approved' list? Who has visited the establishment to check suitability? Does the employer have adequate insurance or is this something that the educational establishment will provide? Are there any specific health and safety requirements?

- *Check that the responsibilities of the student, parent or guardian, local authority, employer and educational establishment are clear.* How does the placement impact on the Every Child Matters agenda? Clear procedures are needed so that everyone knows what the consequences are if a student does not attend, is injured or finds the placement unsuitable.

- *Clearly identify expectations.* Be clear about what learning outcomes will be addressed by the work placement and identify appropriate assessment strategies.

- *Monitor the learning.* Ensure that reporting procedures are in place and that the learner is not left feeling vulnerable and unsupported. Will there be someone available at the workplace and in the educational institution to act as mentor and support for the student?

- *Evaluate the work placement.* Overseeing the quality of the work experience is essential if you intend to involve the same employer again. Gather feedback from parents, students, employers, mentors as well as the success of learning outcomes. Is there anything that needs to be changed?

Reflection 4.5

Using the list as a starting point, what else do you think could be added? Are the relevant procedures and personnel in place? How confident are you that students will gain valuable learning?

Reflection 4.6

There are clear benefits for students in work placement learning, but what does the employer and educational establishment gain?

You may have identified some of the following points:

- *Input into the curriculum.* The employer can provide real-world examples, projects and activities for the students which help the course align with real-world employers' needs.
- *Providing equipment or sponsorship.* Employers may be able to donate equipment or sponsor students in their work placements. They may be interested in 'giving back' to local communities through schools, colleges and learning centres.
- *Student motivation.* Visits to companies can be a very effective way of motivating students, including visits to computer-controlled production lines, medical diagnostic centres, call centres and IT support centres.
- *Direct employment.* Employers may be interested in gaining a preview of individuals who will shortly be entering the job market to determine how quickly they learn, how productive they might be, and without the risk and expense of using an employment agency.
- *Additional benefits.* Projects given to the students can be of direct benefit to the hosting organization or community. They can provide insights into new ways of working. Obviously these have to be very carefully managed and thought is required concerning risk, software warranty and intellectual property rights. Where the placement is with a company using highly specialized, bespoke applications this works less well; due to the short duration of most placements, there is often insufficient time for the placement student to learn the necessary skills in those applications. However, it does help the student to gain a flavour of what it is like to work for the company.

Case Study 4.1

John was placed at a local mechanic's garage for his two-week work placement from college. He really enjoyed tinkering about with cars and was pleased to have been placed there. A week before his work experience began, John suffered a knee injury playing American football and was unable to bend his knee or stand for any length of time. He quickly realized that his work experience would have to be put on hold. John went to the garage to explain the situation before his placement began but the manager suggested that instead of delaying the work experience, John could work in the office for the duration of the original placement and return during the school holidays to do the mechanic's part of the job. Since all of his friends would be out of college for the fortnight, John reluctantly agreed.

Upon starting in the garage's office, John was given the task of updating the second-hand vehicle details available for sale on the firm's rather basic website. Web design was a subject that John had covered in his IT classes at college and he diligently spent the first day designing a new home page and quizzing the manager on what products and services the company would like the site to advertise. The manager was not very sure but agreed to the functionality that John suggested. For the remainder of the fortnight, John was happily employed in the office loading photographs and details of the second-hand cars onto the website. The new website looked professional and the manager liked it. He offered John a Saturday job to continue the work he had started and to devise a new system that would automatically send out MoT and service reminders to existing customers.

It is easy to see from this case study and Case Study 3.3 how the ability to use common applications can be useful in all manner of different situations and can help reduce the workload of people in a variety of industries.

Reflection 4.7

What can you do to help create and sustain partnerships with local businesses? Make a list of all the places that may be suitable and contact them to ask if they are considering offering any work experience places. Look at the projects and resources that you use in the classroom – how close are they to the kind of work that students will meet in the workplace? Do they rely on following instructions or do they help to develop cognitive thinking skills too?

Reflection 4.8

Create a database of all the local employers that may be interested in offering IT work placements and/or apprenticeships. Look at the website for education business partnerships (http://www.iebe.org.uk/index.php/ebpo-directories) to see how other education establishments have organized their work placements. Contact your local careers advisors or Connexions careers website (http://www.connexions-direct.com)

to see what opportunities are local to your establishment. Be proactive – getting someone from industry to explain their job to your students may be a great way of enthusing them.

The synergistic relationship between business and education is further demonstrated at higher education level. Computer science degree programmes are narrowing the technical issues caused by the time lag, discussed in Chapter 3, between the IT systems available in institutions and those in use in business and industry through working more closely. However, according to E-Skills UK (2009c), the programmes also need to produce students with appropriate business acumen, communication and interpersonal skills for the workplace after graduating. 'Evidence from employers and universities indicates that one of the best ways of developing these "business-ready" skills is through professional placements, or internships' (E-Skills UK 2009c). They are currently in a pilot phase and the scheme is being prepared to be launched in late 2010.

Internships have been designed to incorporate the needs of industry and business in addition to the academic rigour required by the university. Typically students will undertake a one-year internship where they will be able to study aspects of the IT sector which would not be possible in the majority of educational institutions, such as risk management, project management and outsourcing. The aim is to provide students with an opportunity to enrich their technical, interpersonal and business skills and to develop a set of skills and capabilities that are widely valued by employers across the IT sector. After graduation the employability of the students will be enhanced and businesses are likely to benefit too as they will be able to recruit the best internship performers to positions in either their graduate programmes or directly into their businesses without incurring recruitment costs and reducing the need for staff induction and orientation into the workplace.

It is also hoped that universities can use internship programmes to attract more students as a result of the sector-wide support of employers to the scheme.

Summary of Key Points

- Digital literacy can be viewed simply as a functional skill, but also as a means to access information and create new and innovative knowledge.
- The digital divide is narrowing, but for those who are marginalized it is becoming deeper.
- There is a need to finding ways to motivate students to get involved in IT at GCSE level and to continue to learn the subject if the knowledge-based society is to be realized.
- Initial work placements are often the seed for a growing relationship between an academic institution and employers, resulting in significant benefits for both.
- Work placements are increasingly being valued as a means of creating opportunities to upgrade students' skills so that they are more valuable to industry and business.

Further reading

Connexions careers website. http://www.connexions-direct.com (accessed 12 January 2010).

CC4G website. http://www.cc4g.net/ (accessed 15 January 2010).

E-Skills UK apprenticeships website. http://www.e-skills.com/apprenticeships (accessed 20 December 2009).

Video and resources for Diploma and internship programme work placements. http://backtoschool.e-skills.com/diploma/ (accessed 12 February 2010).

5

IT qualifications

In this chapter we will focus on:

- Examples of qualifications from entry level to above level 4.
- Assessment methods associated with different qualifications, along with intended target audiences.
- The main qualifications relevant to the IT sector (age 14+).

The loss of many low-skilled jobs in Britain has produced a need for the current workforce to upgrade its skills and for future generations of workers to have a higher standard of skills when leaving the education system. In the not too distant future, the school system in England will see an overhaul with respect to the education leaving age: from 2013 the leaving age will be raised to 17, and from 2015 young people will remain in education until the age of 18. This means that our services as teachers will be in even greater demand, but what is it that we will be teaching?

Many youngsters prefer to follow apprenticeships, continuing their education during day release classes. National Vocation Qualifications (**NVQs**) are likely to play a more significant role due to the vocational nature of apprenticeships. As discussed in Chapter 2, IT is encroaching on more and more areas of our lives and so, as IT teachers, it is likely that our services will be required to support students who are taking subjects other than IT; for example, students of animal care need IT skills to present their portfolios and to access online ordering systems.

For IT as a subject in its own right, there are many courses available to our students, from entry level up to degree and postgraduate levels. This chapter looks at a variety of courses at each level, outlining target audiences, modes of delivery, means of assessment and the number of guided learning hours (**GLH**). This is not intended as an exhaustive list as new courses will replace existing courses as time and needs evolve.

Entry-level qualifications

Entry-level certificates are available through providers such as AQA, City and Guilds, EdExcel, OCR, the National College of Further Education (**NCFE**) and Welsh Joint

Education Committee (**WJEC**). These certificates have slightly different names (some coming under the functional skills ICT banner), but they are essentially practically based courses which serve beginners very well. Transferable skills such as opening files, saving files, printing and font alterations make up part of the word-processing element of all of these qualifications, for example. These skills are reused in other elements, forming a sound basis for tackling higher qualifications.

Achievement at this level provides sufficient knowledge for a learner to progress to a level 1 course (see the next section for further details). The total number of GLH is expected to be less than 50 per course for an entry-level qualification.

These are very flexible qualifications, not aimed at any one particular type of learner; they are a useful first step for all IT users, from pre-GCSE students in schools, through all age ranges and careers to the retired elderly. Once mastered, these functional skills are universally applicable and thus are useful for school-age students, low-skilled workers and first-time users alike.

Case Study 5.1

Sanjay was teaching IT at his local adult education centre. He ran many different courses but the only entry-level course was 'Computers for Beginners'. He ran one of these classes per week with 12 enrolled students. When he had been teaching the course for a few weeks, he was amazed at the variety of the backgrounds his students came from: among the students in his class were a 19-year-old who had left school with no qualifications, a factory worker who was about to be made redundant and needed some basic computer skills to be a viable contender in the job market, an elderly lady who wanted to be able to stay in touch with relatives overseas, and a man who had been forced into early retirement through bad health and wanted to use the computer for online shopping and social networking.

The diversity of the groups encouraged Sanjay to advertise the classes to sectors of the community he would otherwise have ignored. At the end of the first course, all of the students had achieved their qualification and were looking to progress on to a level 1 functional skills ICT course through the adult education centre. In addition to this success, his advertising brought in enough students to run three classes for the entry-level certificate the following year.

Reflection 5.1

What courses other than level 1 functional skills might Sanjay have advised his students to progress following their completion of 'Computing for Beginners'?

There are many other entry-level courses taught throughout Britain, in adult education centres, prisons, skills centres and residential homes. These courses, although without certification, are not without merit. They are a gentle introduction for many into the IT world without being too onerous a commitment of time or money. Many underconfident first-time users seek out courses such as 'Computers for Beginners' or 'Internet for the Terrified', before they learn basic skills and gain confidence and develop the motivation to take their studies further.

Level 1 qualifications

Functional skills ICT level 1 has been offered by 11 different awarding bodies during the two-year pilot of the qualification. This course, in conjunction with functional skills maths and English, was designed to enable learners to develop skills which are both relevant to, and useful in, everyday life. A functional skills ICT qualification reassures prospective employers of a candidate's ability to competently perform common basic IT tasks. It is relevant to all ages as preparation for accessing higher-level courses. The vision of functional skills ICT is to begin to fill in part of Britain's skills gap which should, in turn, increase the productivity of the nation, promoting enterprise and competitiveness (as a population competent in ICT will be able to apply technologies to an ever expanding range of tasks).

ECDL Essentials is a modular IT qualification whose modules map directly to the Information Technology Qualification (**ITQ**) and thus can form the basis of a more comprehensive IT qualification even when the students did not initially set out to accomplish anything more than to provide themselves with basic computer knowledge. ECDL has always been seen as a benchmark qualification in IT and has become easily recognizable by employers. Due to its modular structure, it is very popular with adult learners as additional modules can be added over time, as and when commitments allow.

GCSE/International General Certificate Secondary Education (IGCSE) ICT is aimed mainly at students aged 14–16. The specifications were rewritten in order to engage today's students who have grown up in a more digital age, meaning that the use of the available technologies is now second nature to them. Following unease in the education system around unsupervised coursework, controlled assessment has taken over and this accounts for up to 60 per cent of the final mark. On the written (traditional exam style) paper, there is a mixture of multiple-choice, short-answer and extended-answer questions. Assessments take place more than once per year, but at fixed times.

There is common ground between functional skills ICT and GCSE ICT, and curriculum time can be saved by co-teaching the overlapping areas. This reduces teaching time in schools and allows for more time to be spent on exploring the practical side of ICT and its application to real-world jobs. This will be one of the first qualifications to promote the use of more recent technologies such as social networking, blogging and multi-function devices (Chapter 2 has further details on the latter).

GCSE ICT also offers the opportunity to take a short course rather than a full course. The only difference between the two is the number of modules completed; there is no difference in the level of difficulty, and some modules are compulsory for both awards. To further enhance the flexibility of GCSE IT, there is also a GCSE in Applied ICT which is a double award (i.e. counts as two GCSEs). There is now less difference between Applied GCSE IT and GCSE IT since the GCSE IT has recently been rewritten. Historically, however, GCSE Applied IT was the more practical of the two qualifications.

The awarding bodies that currently offer GCSE/IGCSE accreditation are AQA, Council for the Curriculum Examination and Assessment (**CCEA**), Cambridge International Examinations (**CIE**), EdExcel, International Curriculum and Assessment Agency (**ICAA**), OCR and WJEC. There is a list of exam boards and their website addresses at the end of this chapter.

CLAiT is offered by OCR and although it is solely a level 1 qualification there are two options: level 1 Certificate for IT Users and level 1 Diploma for IT Users. The difference is similar to that found in the GCSE short and full courses, that is, in terms of the quantity rather than the difficulty. In order to achieve the Certificate a student must complete three units (out of a total of eight) and for the Diploma an additional two units are required. For the Certificate and Diploma, Unit 1 is compulsory (as it is seen as demonstrating the candidate's ability to operate both hardware and software components of a typical, modern computer workstation which are necessary to complete the subsequent units).

The **Foundation Diploma in IT** is perhaps the newest qualification to be offered to school-age students (14–19 years). The Diploma is presented as an alternative choice of qualification to GCSEs and A levels. The new features of this qualification are an obligatory work experience (or a series of short work experiences) and a student-led project. This is more a vocationally focused course, with greater emphasis on the use of IT in people's jobs rather than a heavily theoretical course. Through the project and work experience, the Diploma aims to teach young people how technology helps us to function on a day-to-day basis and to look beyond their own (perhaps limited) use of modern-day technological appliances and to identify additional applications for their existing skills.

NVQs of all levels were designed to reflect the competences that people require for their everyday work. Each candidate is assigned an assessor by the education provider and, by mutual agreement between the candidate and the assessor, a programme of work is developed. There is no formal examination associated with NVQs – instead a portfolio of evidence is compiled throughout the duration of the course to demonstrate the requisite skills and knowledge.

Any candidate wishing to work towards an NVQ must have a place of employment from which to base their observations and case studies. This usually precludes those under 16 from working towards NVQ as work placements for this age group can be difficult to find. Due to the flexible nature of an NVQ, there are mandatory units reflecting the core skills of the subject and a choice of optional units which together achieve accreditation. The choice of optional units is influenced by the candidate's employment; for example, for ITQ level 1 (ITQ is the NVQ for the IT sector), it may be appropriate for the choice of optional modules to allow the candidate to either try out new areas of IT or to gain their certification based solely upon their current skills.

Instead of having a specific number of GLH, NVQs must be completed within a specified time period. The timeframe is typically agreed between candidate and assessor, reflects other demands upon the candidate's time, and often differs from candidate to candidate. If the NVQ is not completed within the designated timeframe, extensions may be given but there is a deadline by which time the course must be completed.

There are a myriad of other level 1 courses provided by the different examination boards (as listed at the end of this chapter) and new courses are written and offered as needs dictate. The courses are now (and will continue to be) of different lengths, depending upon their content. The availability of the courses will be demand-driven and is likely to be adaptable to different situations in order to convert generic qualifications into bespoke ones by the inclusion of specific modules. Obviously the more GLH a course requires, the longer it is likely to take the candidate to complete. At level 1, most of the courses are centred around the students being able to use a variety of software applications at a basic user level. For example, a level 1 word-processing assignment for any of the qualifications discussed above would expect the student to be able to perform editing functions such as cut, copy, paste, underline, and embolden, italicize as well as to save, open, close and print a document. Table 5.1 gives a summary of some of the commonly available qualifications at level 1.

Case Study 5.2

Martha's friends and family joined together to buy her a laptop for her retirement. Martha hadn't really wanted one, but felt guilty about the amount of money that had been spent on her, so she signed up for a beginners' class in computing. To make the ordeal more bearable, Martha encouraged a couple of friends to accompany her to the class.

The class was of a mixed age who were all attending for different reasons (much like Sanjay's class in Case Study 5.1) and, although from different backgrounds, they all chatted before the class began and during the break. The work covered in the session was both fun and manageable and this was a pleasant surprise for Martha, but she still knew that computing was not for her.

All three women, however, signed up for a second term of classes and began to complete modules of ECDL Essentials. Before long, Martha was taking an interest in the uses to which her grandchildren put their computers and signing up for yet more classes. By the time Martha and her friends had completed ECDL Advanced, they were holding small classes in residential and care homes and helping out in the beginners' class in which they themselves had started off.

Reflection 5.2

Is there further progression that Martha and her friends might make in developing and using their IT skills?

Level 2 qualifications

In the main, level 2 qualifications follow neatly on from the level 1 qualifications. CLAiT moves up to **CLAiT Plus**, ECDL Essentials progresses to ECDL Extra, GCSE at foundation level has a level 2 partner in GCSE at higher level; there are

Table 5.1 Example level 1 qualifications

Qualification	Target audience	Assessment method	Awarding body	Approximate GLH
CLAiT	Post compulsory	E-assessment Practical demonstration/assignment	OCR	Certificate – 60 Diploma – 100
ECDL Essentials	Post compulsory	Aural/oral/written examination Multiple-choice questions Portfolio Practical demonstration/assignment Task-based controlled assessment	BCS	Certificate – 42 Award – 65
Foundation Diploma	14–19	Varied – dependent upon exam board	AQA City and Guilds EdExcel OCR	600
Functional Skills ICT	14+	Task-based controlled assessment	Award Scheme Development and Accreditation Network (**ASDAN**) ASCENTIS AQA City and Guilds EdExcel Education Development International (**EDI**) NCFE National Open College Network (**NOCN**) OCR Vocational Training Charitable Trust (**VTCT**) WJEC	45

(Continued Overleaf)

Table 5.1 *(Continued)*

Qualification	Target audience	Assessment method	Awarding body	Approximate GLH
GCSE (Foundation) ICT	14–16	Task-based controlled assessment Written examination	AQA CCEA EdExcel International Curriculum and Assessment Agency Exam (**ICAAE**) OCR WJEC	Short course – 60 Full course – 120 Double award – 180
ITQ	all ages	Coursework Portfolio of evidence E-assessment Practical demonstration/assignment Multiple-choice questions Task-based controlled assessment	BCS City and Guilds EdExcel EDI NOCN OCR	Award – 60 Certificate – 100 Diploma – 275

functional skills awards at level 2, ITQ level 2s and Higher Diplomas, together with qualifications which appear for the first time at level 2 such as BTEC awards. Many of these awards do not have level 1 as a pre-requisite but may encompass the teaching of the level 1 material to consolidate a preliminary part of the course. It is worth noting here that any material prepared for a level 1 course can be used as revision or foundation material at the beginning of the corresponding topic in a level 2 course.

A more recent innovation than the ECDL for IT has been the 'E-Skills Passport'. As discussed, the notion of 'essential IT skills' differs from job to job and, with a modular qualification (where the modules are chosen by the candidate), an employer needs the breakdown of the qualification in order to be able to assess whether or not an applicant has the relevant skills for a given job. Whilst one may assume that a person presenting a CLAiT certificate must have covered some form of word processing, spreadsheets or databases, it is possible to choose modules which do not touch on any of those areas. The idea behind the passport was that it acts as an official record of the modules achieved by the individual as both a written document (which can be presented to a prospective employer) and as an online tool holding the most up-to-date information available on the candidate.

The passport system is organized by E-Skills UK, which is part of the Skills for Business network, and as such is not restricted to a single awarding body. Using the National Qualification Framework, it spans units from all major IT qualifications (at the appropriate levels) such that learners can gain credit for competencies demonstrated elsewhere on an entirely new qualification without the need to repeat proven skills.

The **Information Technology Qualification** is a flexible qualification, and the length of time needed to complete it can vary dramatically. Similarly to when ECDL first appeared, expert users attended test centres and passed all modules in a matter of hours (it is possible for an IT expert to qualify in one day on ITQ). Clearly newer IT students will take longer, but ITQ is a qualification (being modular in structure) that can be added to as time and funding allow (rather than having to be completed within one academic year).

The ITQ has been designed to meet the IT needs of businesses, and has a realistic feel to it. Tasks are intended to reflect how people use IT in everyday jobs and, rather than needing technical skills, candidates should find usage skills more than adequate. Under the ITQ, there are unique offerings such as the specialist software units in which IT skills not usually taught in schools, colleges and other educational establishments can be given the credit they deserve. Traditional IT qualifications such as CLAiT and ECDL tended to focus on office/administrative IT skills such as word processing, spreadsheets and databases and have had limited assessment options. Coming from an NVQ background, ITQ promises to offer a variety of assessment methods appropriate to the candidate including oral assessment, e-assessment, portfolio of evidence, written examination and controlled task-based assessment. This sets it apart from qualifications such as CLAiT where controlled assessment is the only recognized form of assessment.

The **Higher Diploma in IT** is one of the choices at level 2 for school-age students (equivalent to GCSEs at A⋆–C grades) and is a two-year course usually taken in place of GCSEs. At all three levels (Foundation, Higher and Advanced), the Diploma is focused on three main themes: Business, People and Technology. Rather than only studying how to use the technologies, as in qualifications such as CLAiT and ECDL, the Diploma aims to investigate how the IT sector functions and discusses the issues surrounding it. Where at the Foundation Diploma level, an assignment could be to use IT to help to run a local club or group by keeping lists of members' details or income/outgoings sheets, at the Higher Diploma level students will go deeper into the project management side of business by writing forward plans and carrying out scheduling tasks, all with the use of IT. The emphasis in this Diploma is fundamentally different from other level 2 courses as it is aimed at school-age students who have grown up with the newer technologies. The Diploma takes the business side of IT so seriously that its creators approached many major employers for content contributions to keep the workplace focus (companies such as British Telecom, Cisco, John Lewis, IBM and Vodafone). Indeed, the Diploma Development Partners which devised the Diplomas are largely populated by employers.

Table 5.2 gives a summary of example qualifications available at level 2.

Case Study 5.3

Petra suffered serious illnesses during her childhood and consequently spent much time in hospital where she needed to keep fairly still. Her parents purchased a laptop computer for her with some games to entertain her. Throughout her treatment and recovery Petra worked her way through various games to stave off the boredom and also investigated other software which had come with the laptop and found that she enjoyed using the word-processing software most.

As she played with the software more and more, her skills base developed and she branched out into desktop publishing software, where she created a recipe book (with favourite recipes from the children on the ward) to sell in order to raise funds for her hospital ward.

Petra was out of school for a year and had to catch up on the academic work she had missed, and whilst she never fully recovered her confidence in maths or English, it was clear that her talents lay in the world of IT. When the time came to choose which educational route to follow at the age of 14, it was an obvious choice for Petra to take the Diploma where she could not only shine, but also begin to learn business applications for the IT skills she already had. She ultimately put her talents to excellent use with a job coming directly from her work experience placement in a web design company.

Reflection 5.3

What advice would you give Petra about what she might do to further her professional development in a web design role?

Table 5.2 Example level 2 qualifications

Qualification	Target audience	Assessment method	Awarding body	Approximate GLH
BTEC – IT Specialist	Post compulsory	Internal verification of various methods deemed to be appropriate to the candiate	EdExcel	Award – 60 Certificate – 120 Extended certificate – 180
CLAiT Plus	Post compulsory	Practical demonstration/assignment	OCR	Certificate – 90 Diploma – 150
ECDL	Post compulsory	Aural/oral/practical/written examination Multiple-choice questions Portfolio of evidence, coursework E-assessment Practical demonstration/assignment Task-based controlled assessment	BCS	ECDL Extra – 120 ECDL Part 2 – 90
Higher Diploma	14–19	Varied – dependent upon exam board	AQA City and Guilds EdExcel OCR	850
Functional Skills ICT	14+	Task-based controlled assessment	ASDAN ASCENTIS AQA City and Guilds EdExcel EDI NCFE NOCN OCR VTCT WJEC	45

(Continued Overleaf)

Table 5.2 (Continued)

Qualification	Target audience	Assessment method	Awarding body	Approximate GLH
GCSE (Higher) ICT	14–16	Task-based controlled assessment Written examination	AQA CCEA EdExcel ICAAE OCR WJEC	Short course – 60 Full course – 120 Double award – 180
ITQ	all ages	Coursework Portfolio of evidence E-assessment Practical demonstration/assignment Multiple-choice questions Task-based controlled assessment	BCS City and Guilds EdExcel EDI NOCN OCR	Award – 75 Certificate – 125 Diploma – 280

Level 3 qualifications

As with many level 2 courses being direct progressions from level 1 courses, the families also extend to level 3. CLAiT Plus moves up to CLAiT Advanced, ECDL Extra goes on to ECDL Advanced, and there is an Advanced Diploma in IT which follows on from the work done in the Higher Diploma. ITQ level 3 continues in the same vein as it did at levels 1 and 2, being modular in structure and with students able to opt in and out of them as required. The flexibility of different assessment methods is still available in ITQ level 3, as is the option to tailor the selection of modules to each individual candidate. Another feature of the ITQ (which is available at every level but is perhaps most relevant at level 3) is that it is available in different 'sizes' at each level – Award, Certificate or Diploma – depending on how many credits have been accumulated: for example, the Award at level 3 requires 12 credits, but the Certificate necessitates 25.

There is a new qualification at level 3 with no lower-level partner, and that is General Certificate of Education (**GCE**) A-level IT. This comes in two sizes, AS level and A level, where again the amount of work is the distinguishing feature. There are also different 'flavours' of GCE: ICT, Applied ICT and Computing with different parts of the IT world emphasized in each. Computing, for example, focuses more on programming than the other qualifications at this level, whilst Applied ICT is available to study as a single or double award (one or two AS or A levels). Table 5.3 shows examples of some of the level 3 qualifications available.

Case Study 5.4

Max would like to go to university and study computer programming and become a software developer (to gain employment as a computer games designer). He had taken the GCSE double award in ICT but decided he needed to focus more on the programming side of IT. He decided to do A levels in Computing, Maths and Business as these would support his degree choice. Max really enjoyed the computing A level and was able to choose modules from the maths A level that deepened his understanding of some of the topics needed in Computing. Friends of his chose to do the other ICT-based A-level courses as they thought Computing to be old-fashioned, but Max had made the right decision and achieved a place at his desired university on a computer science course based on his A-level subjects.

Reflection 5.4

Consider other IT degree programmes. Which combination of IT courses at levels 2 and 3 would best equip students for their degree-level studies?

Level 4 and above qualifications

Upon completion of level 3 qualifications, it is often the case that students go on to study for a degree or similar qualification (such as Higher National Certificate and

Table 5.3 Example level 3 qualifications

Qualification	Target audience	Assessment method	Awarding body	Approximate GLH
BTEC – IT Specialist	Post compulsory	Aural/oral/practical/written examination Multiple-choice questions Portfolio of evidence, coursework E-assessment Practical demonstration/assignment Task-based controlled assessment	EdExcel	Award – 60 Certificate – 175 Diploma – 345
CLAiT Advanced	Post compulsory	Practical demonstration/assignment	OCR	Certificate – 180 Diploma – 300
ECDL Advanced	Post compulsory	Aural/oral/practical/written examination Multiple-choice questions Portfolio of evidence, coursework E-assessment Practical demonstration/assignment Task-based controlled assessment	BCS	220
Advanced Diploma	14–19	Varied – dependent upon exam board	AQA City and Guilds EdExcel OCR	1100
GCE	16–19	Coursework Written examination	AQA CCEA EdExcel OCR WJEC	AS – 180 A level – 360 Double award – 720
ITQ	all ages	Coursework Portfolio of evidence E-assessment Practical demonstration/assignment Multiple-choice questions Task-based controlled assessment	BCS City and Guilds EdExcel EDI NOCN OCR	Award – 90 Certificate – 190 Diploma – 300

Higher National Diploma). Degrees and the like can be completed in a variety of different ways including full-time study, part-time study (requiring day release or more frequent attendance), studying at a university/college or distance learning. Each educational establishment offers different content in its courses, and careful research is required to find the right course (and a suitable learning provider) for a candidate. By the time one has employment commitments (and possibly family commitments too), it can be difficult to find the time to study full-time and to travel to lectures, which is when distance learning becomes a real consideration for many. For those needing to look at distance learning, the Open University offer a plethora of courses from levels 4 to 8 which can all be completed in small sections from home. Table 5.4 gives some of the examination board website addresses.

Table 5.4 Examination board websites

Examination Board		Website Address
ASCENTIS	A national awarding body	http://www.ascentis.co.uk
AQA	Assessment and Qualifications Alliance	http://www.aqa.org.uk
BCS	The Chartered Institute for IT	http://www.bcs.org
CCEA	Council for the Curriculum, Examinations and Assessment	http://www.rewardinglearning.org.uk
CIE	University of Cambridge International Examinations	http://www.cie.org.uk
City and Guilds	The City and Guilds of London Institute	http://www.city-and-guilds.co.uk
EdExcel	Part of Pearson	http://www.edexcel.com
EDI	Education Development International	http://www.ediplc.com
ICAA	International Curriculum and Assessment Agency	http://www.icaa.com
NCFE	Northern Council for Further Education	http://www.ncfe.org.uk
NOCN	National Open College Network	http://www.nocn.org.uk
OCR	Oxford Cambridge and RSA Examinations	http://www.ocr.org.uk
SQA	Scottish Qualifications Authority	http://www.sqa.org.uk
VTCT	Vocational Training Charitable Trust	http://www.vtct.org.uk
WJEC	Welsh Joint Education Committee	http://www.wjec.co.uk

Summary of Key Points

- There is a wide range of courses available at each level appropriate to the needs of individual learners.
- Courses may be accredited or non-accredited, whilst still contributing to an overall qualification.
- Different progression routes are available to suit a range of learners.

6

Teaching and learning strategies

In this chapter we will focus on:

- Some of the reasons for mixing more experiential and activity-based learning with traditional teaching methods used in IT.
- The importance of information skills and the reflective process in the development of cognitive skills required for problem-solving and creativity.
- Skills and characteristics of learners enrolled on pre-entry to level 4 and above IT programmes.
- Inclusive strategies for differentiated learning, identifying readily available **assistive technology**.
- Health and safety aspects of using IT, including the optimization of classroom layout and the development of an e-safety policy.

Marc Prensky (2001) and Stephen Heppell (http://www.heppell.net) are influential figures in the debate about the embedding of IT-based pedagogies into teaching; the use of so-called information learning technology (ILT). This duality of roles for teachers of subjects other than IT can be quite daunting as they learn to manage and deal effectively with their main subject and then embed additional IT skills into their teaching tool-kit. IT teachers might, on the other hand, appear to have an easier task – not only teaching their main subject, but also doing so through the medium of IT, often being viewed as 'experts' in their field. However, this pedagogy can have a disadvantage as teaching IT solely through the medium of IT-based methodologies and strategies can make the learning strategies rather one-dimensional and possibly uninteresting. Chapter 7 gives examples of how mixed pedagogies can work in the teaching of IT. We believe IT teachers can successfully overcome such problems by incorporating examples of teaching strategies from other curriculum areas to mix with IT pedagogies to add changes of pace and focus in lessons, such as guided discovery learning and role play. It is also important to mix the strategies to embed inclusive teaching practices and to create opportunities for differentiation and to engage all learning styles.

Towards IT integration

In Chapter 4 we described how IT literacy should not be viewed simply as a set of functional skills, though many of the qualifications available up to level 3 stress the assessment of such skills. Instead, as Kuhlthau (1987) and others have emphasized, IT literacy should be seen not simply as a discrete set of functional skills, but rather as a process of thinking and learning. The fully conversant IT literate person needs to combine functional understanding with more fundamental, structural understanding of what is going on and to be able to locate relevant information to create new knowledge that can then be expressed in an appropriate manner. Such a person will therefore need to integrate not only functional skills, but also information and media skills that are superimposed upon personal characteristics such as confidence and self-motivation. These are summarized in Figure 6.1.

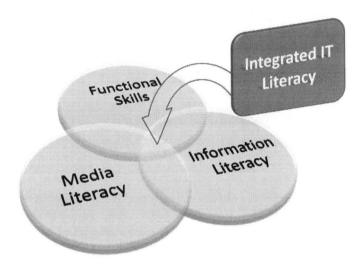

Figure 6.1 Integrated IT literacy as a combination of functional skills, information literacy and media literacy

The learners we are hoping to develop are those who feel able to integrate all three abilities. They will be much more likely to be independent learners and enquirers who will be best equipped to undertake the challenges of embedding IT successfully in the workplace, in society and for their own recreation. Such learners will be more likely to develop appropriate criticality and thinking skills, recognize more easily the consequences of actions and constructively question the actions of others. These 'higher' skills form the scaffolding required to create learners with abilities to problem-solve, innovate and create new knowledge.

Eisenberg and Berkowitz (1990) developed the 'Big Six Skills approach', to information problem-solving across multiple conditions. The framework provides a systematic structure through which teachers can assist learners to develop the necessary cognitive skills for solving problems. Such critical thinking skills, when combined with functional and media literacies, can also be applied to IT challenges. However, rather than the processes being linear, we prefer to think of them as forming a reflective cycle (Figure 6.2) that enhances the process of metacognitive learning, defined by Phelps *et al.* (2001 p. 481) as that which 'empowers learners to become more independent in their approach to learning with, and about, computers in the future' and which promotes 'the development of individuals capable of life-long computer learning'.

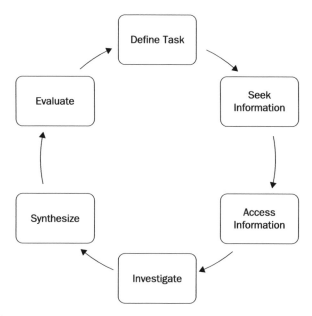

Figure 6.2 Critically reflective cycle based on the Big Six Skills approach (Eisenberg and Berkowitz, 1990)

Applying the Big Six Skills approach to IT problem-solving, the following stages can be extrapolated.

Define the task. Ensure that the question or problem is understood and clarify if necessary. Determine what IT application is most suitable. What kind of information is needed and to what depth, which media do you need to refer to or use in the task?

Seek information. Use a **mind-map** or similar technique to investigate what can be used to solve the task either individually or with colleagues. Select the most appropriate.

Access information. Conduct the appropriate research to find the sources of information required. Does your initial research lead you to any additional sources that could be included? Where are you going to look for the information?

Investigate. Connect with the research by reading the relevant articles, watching videos, discussing the topic, listening to colleagues. Be selective at this stage and determine what to keep and what to discard. Make notes using applications such as Microsoft **OneNote** or create a folder in which to keep all the relevant information and source references.

Synthesize. Compile the information in the appropriate format. Classify the type of information. Make new knowledge and links between the information, ensuring that information is fully referenced. Check that your chosen format and level is suitable for your audience. Create a draft and check it before producing the final product. Check that you have answered the original question.

Evaluate. Reflect on the final result. Gather feedback if possible from colleagues and audience. What went well and why? What could be improved for the next task? What have you learned from this task about the process of problem-solving? What will you do differently next time?

Reflection 6.1

Reflect on your own teaching. Describe a teaching situation where you have demonstrated each of these six aspects.

We are not suggesting that everyone will invent the equivalent of Sir Tim Berners-Lee's internet by following this methodology. However, we do suggest that if such notions of critical reflection are part of a teacher's embedded values and ethos then such ideas are more likely to become an intrinsic part of how students learn to learn. With such skills a student is more likely to feel empowered and to apply their learning more creatively. In the next part of this chapter we will look at this process in more detail.

Learner skills and characteristics

Entry level

Due to the dynamic nature of IT, students who set out on IT foundational courses will exhibit a very wide range of ability in terms of functional skills, media literacy and information literacy. At foundation level, more mature students – Prensky's 'digital immigrants' – are likely to have either no experience of IT at all or a mix of self-taught skills, peer learning and basic courses. This book is for those who teach a broad age range of students, and it is worth remembering that while the majority of students aged up to 25 are likely to have been using computers to learn from an early age, more mature students are much more likely to have been educated using textbooks.

Adult education classes such as 'Computers for the Terrified' and 'Computing from Scratch' are designed for learners with little or no experience in IT in terms of functional skills, but they may be highly adept at information literacy and/or some aspects of media literacy. Entry-level qualifications were discussed in Chapter 5. Foundation courses for younger students, or perhaps those first starting out on their Diplomas in IT or GCSEs, will most likely have already benefited from using IT at school and been exposed to IT from an early age – Prensky's so-called 'digital natives'. They will also be likely to have taught themselves some of the principles of IT or learnt from their peers from a young age.

In either case learners are highly likely at this stage to have a very 'spiky profile' (a term borrowed from literacy and numeracy curricula). This profile describes how a student may be highly literate in, for example, searching the internet and using a mobile phone, but has gaps in their knowledge of computer hardware or how to use presentation software. Students will also have very different aspirations and motivations for undertaking IT courses, so it is important to understand what a learner may be interested in, in order to enthuse them in the learning process. Whatever the learning situation and whatever preconceptions the teacher may have about the student's abilities, initial assessment should underpin any learning plan. Teachers using IT must always also be aware of any additional support that may be required in terms of assistive technology, as described later in this chapter. Initial and other suggested assessment methodologies are discussed further in Chapter 8.

Everything that we have mentioned in terms of spiky profiles continues throughout the levels, due to the dynamic nature of IT. New versions and new products enter the commercial world very rapidly and it will be necessary to continually update skills and processes to keep up. Thankfully, many of the skills that we gain are transferable. This means that we can realign learning from one area into another as we recognize, for example, commonality in applications or can identify that the speed of the processor may be one of the reasons for an application being slow to respond. This 'scaffolding' can be further enhanced if the teacher encourages the learners to make connections between different areas of learning. This is sometimes a difficult and time-consuming process, requiring the teacher to be highly conversant with their subject matter and understand the interrelational aspects of the subject. However, time spent on this will pay dividends later and learning will often gather pace towards the middle of the course if sufficient time is spent at the beginning in this way.

Reflection 6.2

Think back to the last software application that you learnt. How did you learn to use it? What skills, knowledge and experience were you able to transfer from previous learning?

Levels 1 and 2

Students in schools and colleges at these levels will most likely be undertaking courses such as foundation learning, Foundation or Higher Diplomas in IT, OCR Nationals or full-time GCSE. For adults this may equate to the ECDL Basics and Extra, ITQ or CLAiT qualifications previously described in Chapter 5 in more detail.

Courses at these levels encourage the memorization of linked pathways to negotiate an assortment of specific software menus to produce a required outcome. Undoubtedly such basic skills are important for the scaffolding of future learning, but there is a huge diversity in what IT is used and how learners already use it in their lives. Therefore, rigorous initial assessment is vital at the beginning of these courses.

Teaching and learning at these levels are mainly centred on the functional skills of learning IT and media applications to produce a desired outcome. Functional literacy such as how to operate a mouse efficiently undoubtedly needs practice and it is vital that such skills become part of an automatic process. In this way the hand–eye co-ordination becomes second nature and frees the mind to think several steps ahead, even allowing time to think of alternatives and to choose between them. The learner can devote more time to higher-order processing than to worrying about techniques and which menu options to choose.

However, if the learning becomes solely about learning menus by rote then it is very likely to disengage learners, and once they have become 'switched off' it is an uphill struggle to re-engage them. This is given as one of the main reasons for the large reduction in the number of students continuing to study IT subjects after level 2 in schools, as discussed in Chapter 4. Unless the learning is contextualized and made relevant to the student the learning process can easily become monotonous and one-dimensional. Contextualizing learning brings the abstract into the real world in terms of how it can be applied to business, the workplace, leisure, entertainment, further learning and administration processes.

Teaching in context and involvement of the students' own interests in the learning are vital in maintaining student attention and motivation, which are necessary to begin the process towards creating an empowered learner who will wish to continue with IT as a subject to a higher level. Strategies often employed at this level involve the use of copying from copious workbooks, worksheets and practice exercises or following didactic demonstrations provided by the teacher. These methods are aimed at encouraging learners to memorize specific menu paths such as the order of the menus needed to change the margins on a word-processed document. Even at this level, however, thinking skills can be stretched by involving the students in determining the subject they wish to word-process. An example would be allowing learners to research their own topic and asking them to produce a word-processed document with margins set at anything other than the default using their own material. This is much more motivating, involves research and synthesis and requires much more cognition than simply copying. This is the students' 'own' piece of work that they have produced and they will want it to look good. If the scripts are then shared with the group, peer learning and evaluation will occur naturally. Students will learn to take risks, try things out for themselves and become more resilient and adaptive if such approaches are encouraged, the more so if the teacher encourages learners to see connections and helps them to identify transferable skills that can be utilized and combined in different ways. More teaching and learning resources are described in Chapter 7.

Level 3

As discussed in Chapter 5, qualifications at this level, especially in schools, have been traditionally based around AS and A level, but there are now more options in the form of the Advanced Diploma in IT and apprenticeships which usually include a work-based qualification. At this level learners should be confident and independent. Alongside functional skills capability, information and media literacies, the aptitude to solve problems needs to be developed ready for the student to investigate more theoretical models and extend their criticality and questioning abilities. Learners at this level need to be curious about the world and how it works so that they can see connections and interrelationships between IT and parts of commerce and industry outside the classroom.

Level 4 and above

As students approach level 4 most will either move into higher or further education to take qualifications such as a degree or become involved in a higher apprenticeship. Those who move into the workplace will most likely continue to take specific technical or professional qualifications. They may choose to specialize or to generalize. By this stage it is hoped that learners will have a theoretical understanding and be able to synthesize and evaluate learning as part of their everyday life. Most learners when moving into the workplace will experience a period where everything appears new and strange but will rapidly adapt to the specific procedures and policies in place and will be able to transfer the skills and knowledge gained from their education into the workplace.

Figure 6.3 summarizes the development of skills across the various levels.

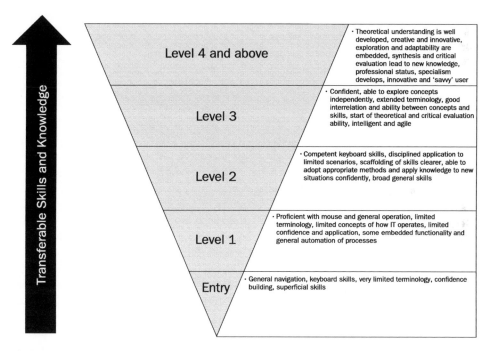

Figure 6.3 Development of skills from entry to level 4 and above

Equality and diversity

Equality and diversity issues and the associated need for differentiation should be a thread through all teaching and learning, and IT is no exception. Indeed, it is even more essential to recognize that not only do we need to differentiate in terms of level of task, support levels, teaching strategy, time allowances and special educational needs, but we also need to be aware that there is an additional variable – one of equipment availability and accessibility. It is imperative to recognize that not all students will have uninterrupted access to relevant computer equipment at home or that all home computers will have identical software and hardware. Research shows that those students who have computer access outside the school are more confident in their use and have a more positive attitude to IT in general compared to those without or with only limited access in the home (Selwyn 1997). For mature students, computer incompatibility may also be a significant barrier to learning at home where they may have purchased second-hand computers with legacy software or not updated their operating system as new releases became available.

Several schools have attempted to overcome compatibility issues through the provision of laptops to children, often as part of a sponsorship deal with manufacturers, and Becta is currently overseeing the Home Access programme. This is a government-led initiative that is intended to benefit more than 270,000 households by March 2011 that currently have no access to IT in the home. The staged rollout across England will initially target families with school children in Years 3–9.

> **Reflection 6.3**
>
> Imagine you are one of your students. How would you like to learn IT? Are you able to rank the importance of confidence, skills, knowledge and experience in any particular order?

Some may argue that perhaps all these attributes should be taught at once in a holistic manner and that they cannot be separated from each other. Others may decide that knowledge is the product of skills and experience and that confidence is needed to endow students with the necessary will to have a go at something new. Every group of students is different and, within each group, each learner will at different times present with different needs. It does not really matter how you get there as long as you do, though generally a group that is at ease and whose confidence is on an upward curve is much more likely to develop better in terms of skills, inquisitiveness, respect for other learners and deeper understanding in any subject. A supportive environment in which confidence can flourish is so often an underrated aspect in teaching. A teacher who is confident enough to say 'I don't know all the answers, but perhaps we can ask others or find out' is more likely to gain the respect of students than one who tries to intimidate or bluff.

Assistive technology

Most operating systems come pre-packaged with assistive technology, and it is essential that teachers are aware of the various functional features available so they can assist students. The options that are available will vary according to the operating system installed on the computer, but some of the most common are described below:

- StickyKeys – allows a student to press Ctrl, Alt and Del keys sequentially rather than simultaneously.

- FilterKeys – reduces keyboarding errors for learners who tend to press the same key in very quick succession.
- SoundSentry – gives a visual message when a sound is played.
- High Contrast – screen outputs can be configured to provide typing and icons in high-contrast colour palettes, reducing eyestrain by improving the contrast between the text and the background.
- MouseKeys – allows a user to direct the mouse direction using the numeric keyboard pad.
- Cursor options – allows the cursor to be made larger, change shape and to alter the blink rate.
- Left-handed mouse – some left-handed learners prefer to use the mouse to the left of the computer and therefore the usual left and right mouse clicks are reversed unless this option is enabled.
- Magnifier – 'magnifying glass' that can be moved over the screen using the mouse to zoom in. It provides a screen within a screen view.
- Narrator – reads desktop icon texts aloud as you pass the mouse over them and verbalizes keystrokes.
- Bespoke assistive software is also available such as voice input software, alongside assistive technology such as adapted keyboards and different types of computer mice such as trackballs.

Reflection 6.4

Do you know how to turn on the accessibility options on your computers? Can you identify what each one does? Do you have easy access to a trackball mouse or adapted keyboard?

Differentiation

In addition to such assistive technologies it is vital that students are given appropriate advice and support. The drop-out rate from IT is an increasing problem especially for young adults, as discussed in Chapter 4. Strong pastoral support through personal tutors and mentoring has been identified as key aspect of maintaining interest and engagement along with appropriate levels of differentiated teaching and learning activities.

Differentiation can be in terms of pace, teaching strategy, level of difficulty, level of support, length of time given, type of task to allow students as much choice as possible on the content of their work while still recognizing the need to evidence the processes used. Remember also those learners who may be more adept at completing tasks and be ready to suggest extensions to any activities for these learners. Here are some suggestions:

- *Pace.* Always be clear about the length of time an activity should take. Plan an activity to take the appropriate time for a student who will take the most time, but add additional points onto the activity. When setting the task introduce it as 'Go as far as point 6, but if you complete that carry on to point 10'.

- *Teaching strategy.* Vary the methods that you use and determine whether you will place learners in groups according to similar ability or whether you will mix the groupings to encourage peer learning.
- *Difficulty level.* Give differentiated groups tasks based on how difficult they are to achieve or the level of quality required for the finished product.
- *Support level.* Set the task to the group and then allow the students to carry on while you give individual attention to some learners or expect some students to research their own topic, give others more starting information or reduce the selection to choose from.
- *Type of task.* Divide a whole-group project into various tasks and assign them to different students based on the level of challenge you need to set them. Bring all the tasks together to make the group project coherent. This type of activity is best set over two or three sessions.

Reflection 6.5

Give an example of how you differentiate in your teaching. Do you record it on your lesson plan? How do you evaluate whether the differentiation was appropriate?

Health and safety

Equipment

The Health and Safety (Display Screen Equipment) Regulations (1992), amended in 2002, require employers to provide suitable visual display units (**VDUs**) and computer equipment for their employees. These regulations do not necessarily apply to learners in educational institutions, though students who are already in the workplace and school children who will increasingly be involved in work placements will need to know these regulations.

Remember that when teaching it is not good practice to work on the screen without a break for more than about 45 minutes. Using group work and mixing teaching strategies will help to break up the lessons into smaller sessions of about 20 minutes each. This will help to reduce eyestrain, improve concentration span and allow time for students to discuss and ask questions. Most of the problems are eliminated by maintaining good posture, good technique and good workstation design. The main points to be aware of are the following:

- *Repetitive strain injury* (**RSI**), which presents as aches and pains in hands, limbs, neck and back. This is mainly due to poor posture. Footrests, appropriately set workstations and adjustable chairs will usually improve the situation.
- *Eyestrain,* which presents as tired or dry eyes, headaches or blurred vision.

Frequent short breaks are recommended as well as eliminating screen glare and incorrectly set monitor controls such as brightness and contrast. Students may need to have an eye test and spectacles for wearing when using VDU equipment. Maintaining correct posture, with eyes relaxed and looking straight forward at the monitor, will also help to minimize eyestrain.

Reflection 6.6

Reflect on your own posture. How do you need to improve your practice? Remember students may unconsciously copy your own bad habits!

Example of health and safety induction activity

Download a free copy of the Health and Safety Executive's leaflet on VDU use from their website (HSE 2006). The internet is also a good source of images.

Set up a workstation with the following equipment deliberately set incorrectly:

- gas lift computer operator's chair with the back and seat height set incorrectly;
- mouse placed on the left-hand side of the screen with wire trailing over keyboard;
- screen tilted (preferably so that it catches the glare of lights) and too low or too high;
- screen contrast set too high;
- keyboard set with feet down and too near the front edge of the table;
- footrest under the desk but to one side;
- drinks can (empty) next to the keyboard.

Divide the class into groups and ask each group to approach the workstation and note what is wrong and how to put it right. Let the groups peer-assess each other's findings and encourage the learners to put the equipment in the right place. In subsequent lessons reinforce the learning from this activity as students continue in other subjects.

Computer room layout

A further health and safety consideration is the layout of the classroom. For many teachers this is a 'given' as network points and electrical cables have often been installed without their input and in many schools and colleges the computer suites have been designed using traditional design skills. Research by Egan *et al.* (2009) from the University of Bedfordshire has indicated that the majority of classrooms used for the teaching of IT in schools are poorly designed and that this can affect both teacher morale and student attainment. Our observations have been that this situation is beginning to improve, particularly in schools, but that many still have a way to go; this is still the case in many further education and adult education classes. According to the research the main issues are the following:

- Poor visibility for at least some of the students, often caused by inappropriate pillars or dividers or long and narrow rooms so the students are unable to see the teacher and projector screen.

- Spacing between workstations is often too narrow to allow students to take notes on the desk space or for the teacher to sit next to a student to give individual support at eye level.

- Unsuitable chairs for the students that are not adjustable to the appropriate height for the desks.

- Unsuitable lighting that causes glare on the screens or makes it difficult to see them clearly.

- Inefficient ventilation usually causing overheating in the room.

- Inappropriate positioning of the projector and whiteboard, which should be ideally situated on the wall along the widest part of the room. Often the whiteboard is also used as the projector screen, and the resulting screen glare causes problems as well as an inability for the teacher to use the whiteboard to summarize points.

- Students being unable to see the teacher or teacher being unable to see the students' screens without difficulty.

- Lack of seating areas for group discussions and for planning and plenary sessions.

The research recommends the following elements to provide an appropriate room arrangement. These are also shown in Figure 6.4:

- Windows above monitor height or window blinds to reduce glare and direct sunlight.

- All chairs adjustable and arranged so students can rotate easily to see the projector.

- Projector and whiteboard on the longest wall.

- Workstation areas set at a minimum width of 600 mm with spacing between workstations at a minimum of 650 mm.

- Desk areas deep enough for suitable positioning of keyboard and mouse to allow students to rest forearms on the desk while using the equipment.

- Additionally, we recommend the provision of group work areas so that students can move positions within the room to undertake various collaborative assignments. This also allows for greater opportunities for differentiation.

Research by Palmer (unpublished) in her school environment determined that the majority of IT classrooms were not purpose-built, simply adapted from normal classrooms. Much of the classroom furniture, such as workstations and chairs, is not designed for computer use. All the rooms were smaller than the ideal classroom size of 80 m^2 advocated by Egan *et al.* (2009) and some had pillars that restricted views and prevented group work from taking place.

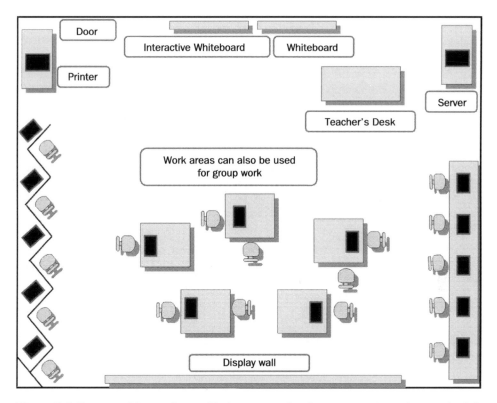

Figure 6.4 Suggested layout for an IT classroom, showing staggered seating on the left following recommendations of Egan *et al.* (2009), or alternative arrangement on the right

Reflection 6.7

Review your own IT classroom layout against the recommendations of the research project. Is there anything that you consider could be improved? Why not involve the students in planning a computer suite – such a project could involve, for example, internet research, project management, surveys, costings, report writing skills, embedding numeracy, use of graphics or design software and presentations.

Creating a safe working environment (e-safety)

Safeguarding children and adults from inappropriate and/or inaccurate internet content and making undesirable contacts through, for example, social networking sites is everyone's responsibility. Internet safety is of growing concern, and some of the potential threats were discussed in Chapter 1. In response the government commissioned the Byron Review (DCSF 2008a) to investigate the potential risks of internet use by children and young people, though the report's recommendations are of equal importance for safeguarding adults. The report recommended that rather than trying to prevent access to the internet, education and information on the risks should be discussed openly to empower adults, children and young people to manage the risks posed by internet in a responsible fashion. As Byron remarks in her Executive Summary (DCSF 2008b, p. 2): 'At a public swimming pool we have gates, put up signs, have lifeguards and shallow ends, but we also teach children how to swim.'

The recommended safeguards include reducing the availability of unsafe and inappropriate material on the most popular websites, using appropriate software such as firewalls, content filters, online panic buttons and anti-virus programs to reduce inappropriate access and to improve what the report termed 'resilience' so that users have the right skills to be able to make confident choices when presented with inappropriate content. The DCSF suggests that internet users should be prepared to 'Zip-it, block-it, flag-it'. This means that we should keep quiet about our personal information, use software to prevent inappropriate material reaching us, and let others know if you think there is a problem.

The IT classroom teacher should not, however, be responsible for setting or primarily managing the e-safety policy of the establishment, though it is likely that they may be asked to become involved in the selection and implementation of software such as virus prevention, filtering and content control packages.

It is the responsibility of senior managers to formulate e-safety principles as an element in a much broader range of policies on acceptable and safe behaviour as part of a whole-establishment approach. By consulting with all interested parties, including all classroom teachers and, where applicable, the local authority, governing body, ISP, teaching support staff, students, parents and guardians, e-safety is much more likely to be accepted and guidance more likely to be followed. The formulation, implementation and review of an acceptable use policy (**AUP**) should be necessary for any educational establishment.

It is no longer the case that the teacher is, along with a recommended list of textbooks, the only source of information and knowledge in educational contexts. In today's world it is vital for the students to be able to evaluate the information available from other sources. Remember that it is easy for anyone to publish almost anything they like on the internet and there is a lot of out-of-date, inaccurate and deliberately misleading information on websites. Any policy needs to consider that learners will also interact with the internet outside the learning establishment, and the devices they use may not be protected by firewalls or content filters. Emphasis needs to be on recognizing the potential risks involved in internet use, and the development of cognitive skills needs to be embedded in learning. Validation of internet sources and an ability to cross-check information are skills that need to be learnt at an early stage. Any e-safety policy should be regularly discussed as part of a teacher's CPD and become a central theme in any learner's educational practice.

Reflection 6.8

How do you make IT students aware of the e-safety aspects of your establishment's AUP? Ask your students to design an e-safety policy for use in your classroom. List three of your wider responsibilities to enforce such policy throughout your establishment.

Summary of Key Points

- Independent learners need more than just functional skills; they also require media and information skills to attain IT integration required by business and commerce.
- Innovative, confident and creative IT teachers encourage critical thinking, reflection, self-motivation and confidence in students.
- Transferable skills and scaffolding of knowledge can be encouraged by knowledge-able and adaptable teachers who keep up to date with their CPD.
- Inclusive learning means that teachers need to become familiar with spiky profiles and learning barriers to embed inclusivity in their learning programmes.
- Safe working practices should be adhered to and reinforced at every opportunity.

Further reading

AbilityNet is a registered charity that gives advice on adaptive technologies and initiatives. http://www.abilitynet.org.uk/ (accessed 20 November 2009).

Becta's schools website gives guidance on e-safety for both inside and outside the school gates. http://schools.becta.org.uk/ (accessed 12 December 2009).

DCSF (2010) *Do We Have Safer Children in the Digital World? A Review of Progress since the 2008 Byron Review.* http://www.dcsf.gov.uk/byronreview/pdfs/do%20we%20have%20safer%20children%20in%20a%20digital%20world-WEB.pdf (accessed 2 May 2010).

Kennewell, S., Parkinson, J. and Tanner, H. (2003) *Learning to Teach ICT in the Secondary School.* Oxford: RoutledgeFalmer.

7

Teaching and learning resources

In this chapter we will focus on:

- Blended teaching and learning strategies, both IT- and non-IT-based.
- The use of experiential learning to promote the integration of IT into everyday lives.
- Using project-based learning to mimic the workplace.
- Encouraging and developing cognitive process-based learning alongside product-based activities.

The authors are very fortunate to have taught in many learning situations: schools, the private sector, prisons and further and higher education, and one has been an assistant IT examiner for one of the examination boards for several years. We have been involved in educating both the motivated and the not so motivated student, working in ideal and not so ideal situations.

We have spent a lot of time observing and supporting teachers on initial teacher training programmes and cannot fail to recognize the breadth and commitment of the majority of these teachers in wishing to produce teaching that is 'special' for their students. Their commitment to trying something different is really encouraging, but it does sometimes take a little investment of time, effort and perseverance to update skills. This mindset is as important for the teacher as it is for the student, as teachers can be as prone to boredom as their students. A learner can identify and will usually react negatively to a bored teacher. We would also encourage experienced teachers to have a look at some of these activities (which are by no means exhaustive) and to evaluate their practice to determine if they could also update the way that they teach.

Teaching IT does not have to be restricted to teaching through the medium of IT. Too often an IT lesson can mean 'one student equals one machine' and that can detract from the importance of having IT as a fully integrated part of life rather than just another academic lesson. Teaching a beginner basic mouse control can be achieved using a simple painting/drawing program, where the idea of drawing with a pencil on paper can be easily translated onto the screen.

We freely admit to being active learners and like to incorporate active teaching strategies into our practice. How many of us only refer to the online manual or CD as a last resort, preferring instead to 'play' with software and equipment first to see how intuitive the product is and if any transferable skills can be used? Whilst it is not the same for everyone, perhaps this mode of learning provides opportunities for students to accept and learn from 'failure' in a supportive environment. Learning from experience is an important part of the learning process that helps to build resilience and self-reliance. Cognitive (thinking) skills can be 'tested' through problem-solving activities, and such methods go a long way towards creating confident, pro-active, autonomous learners rather than passive receivers of content. The difficulties and issues surrounding the assessment of **collaborative projects** are discussed in Chapter 8.

Deployment of some of the activities described in this chapter may be difficult to achieve in all situations due to issues such as firewall or hardware restrictions, but in the main should be manageable using software that is tried and tested and available free to download.

Teaching activities

It is important when introducing any subject to first discuss with students how much they may already know and to involve those students who have some knowledge in the teaching and learning process. With any group, we need to find out what interests them and teach IT from their perspective. This can be achieved by recognizing past learning and helping to contextualize the subject by indicating how others have used it successfully. This comes from well-planned initial and diagnostic assessments, discussed in Chapter 8. It is then important to demonstrate and discuss various aspects of the subject using role play or setting a scenario or case study.

An example of using these **blended learning** activities is the use of a card index system with a list of estate agents before demonstrating its use to achieve a specific outcome.

Case Study 7.1

Databases for many students are not understood particularly intuitively and often require contextualization to promote understanding. Joshua is a new IT teacher and has spent two lessons explaining and demonstrating the purpose of an electronic database to his students, but they are still finding it difficult to understand. Joshua decided to approach his mentor, Olivia, and ask for advice.

Olivia suggested that an excellent way of understanding the difference between sorting and searching would be for the students to perform this activity physically for themselves. She suggested that Joshua could invent a scenario using a card index system for houses (details of which are on sets of cards) which are to be sold by an estate agency and a fictitious family who are looking for a property in the area. The cards could be used in a role play activity and could include details such as:

- number of bedrooms
- parking
- number of bathrooms
- council tax band
- town
- postcode
- preferred date of moving
- price
- type of house

Joshua created the cards and a worksheet with a list of tasks to be completed including activities such as:

- Sort the cards according to the number of bedrooms. How many houses are available with three bedrooms? (ascending/descending numerical sort)
- Sort the cards according to council tax order. How many different council tax bands are there? (ascending alpha sort)
- What is the third most expensive house? (descending currency sort, but this task does not tell the students how to go about the task)
- Find how many flats have three bedrooms.
- Search for houses with four bedrooms and at least two bathrooms. Write down their postcodes. (two-field query using an inequality)
- Write down the postcodes of all properties that fall into the price range £150,000–£200,000 and have a garage. (two-field query using a range)

Joshua found that when it came to the students creating their own databases based on their interests such as a stamp collection or details of a music/film collection, they were able to better understand the concept of sorting and searching within a database.

Reflection 7.1

How could you extend this activity to include other aspects of database use?

With some imagination this activity could be extended in terms of understanding the importance of accurate data entry by including spelling errors on some cards, since humans can still process the data with these errors whereas the computer would not find the match. For example, Chatham misspelt as 'Chatam' would not be included in a computer-generated list searching for 'Chatham'. This activity would highlight the importance of accurate typing and introduce the use of codes into an electronic database to reduce the amount of manual input and mistakes.

Using realia in IT

As IT teachers we need to reinforce the application and uses of what we teach in each and every lesson to keep the subject matter relevant to students. We can look around us and collect realia that will be useful in drawing parallels between the projects we set our students and the application of IT in our technologically advancing world. These may include flyers from the local pizza delivery firm, posters advertising forthcoming social events such as a rock concert or rugby match (to demonstrate different uses of desktop publishing), a card index system or passport application form (to demonstrate how databases may be designed and constructed). Table 7.1 contains some examples of realia which could be used as a starting point to provide links between the IT world and the real world.

Table 7.1   Examples of realia which could be used to introduce topics

Word processing	*E-mail*	*Presentation*
Formal letter	Posted letter	Overhead projector
Instruction leaflet	Fax	Slides
Textbook		Hand-drawn transparencies
Novel		
Database	*Spreadsheet*	*Desktop publishing*
Telephone directory	Stock control sheet	Pizza delivery leaflet
Address book	Balance sheet	Magazine page
Card index system	Statistical presentations	CD inlay
Benefit application form	Order form	Greetings card
Passport application		
Personal organizer	*Blog*	*Photo editing*
Diary	Journal	Postcard
Appointment book	Diary	Photograph album
Calendar	Day book	Family photograph
Address book	Note pad	
Sticky note pad		

Project-based learning

Projects promote collaborative working and encourage students to investigate different ways in which IT can work for them. Learning in this way creates opportunities to practise communication skills and delegation, both vital skills in any work environment. As teachers, we strive to set appropriate and exciting challenges which motivate our learners to explore aspects of IT which are new to them. For some students, this might be something as simple as setting up address labels in a word-processing package so they can print off Christmas card labels each year; for others it might be using social networking sites.

Example project 1

This project is designed for use in a school environment with a class of 14–16-year-olds. The overall objective is to research the feasibility of opening a school tuck shop (with the assumption that a suitable room has already been found for such a purpose).

Consideration will need to be given as to which products are allowed to be sold on school premises because the project is supposed to be authentic (it is not a good idea to focus only on selling chocolate and fizzy drinks) and there should be enough of a range to create a real interest in the project. This could be set as a cross-curricular project working closely with the business, economics, mathematics, art, sports and health departments. The amount of class time and self-study time dedicated to each stage of the project will need to be determined once the abilities of the students have been assessed.

Stage 1 of the project might be to split the class into groups of a manageable size and have them work together to brainstorm their ideas of what should be for sale in the tuck shop; this can be documented in an i-map. At this stage, the groups can each set up a **blog** to which they can all contribute to keep a record of their progress (this can be done on the school **intranet** if security issues and concerns over external access are an issue) or on a VLE.

There is bound to be discussion and dispute over which goods should be sold and it can be suggested to the groups that they undertake a survey in order to canvass opinion from their perspective customers. There are free-to-download survey software programs that can be used to create surveys with a professional look, possibly introducing a new area of IT to students. Students can ask their peers to complete the survey by posting hyperlinks on social networking sites or by including links in their blog which they can create as part of the project. Results of surveys can help to embed numeracy into IT classes by way of frequency charts and other statistical analyses.

Following successful completion of the first stage, each group should have some raw survey results which they can process in stage 2. For more able students there are several different techniques which could be used – for example, **Gantt** charts and scheduling diagrams could be introduced so that groups can divide the tasks up in an efficient manner and acquire the skills necessary to determine the order in which tasks need to be completed.

Whether undertaking the scheduling exercise or not, the results of the survey should be presented (ideally to the whole class) by the students. This introduces the need for each group to create a presentation which will include tabular data and charts representing the survey's findings as well as the usual introductory and conclusion slides. By presenting to the class as a whole, feedback can be given through peer assessment and improvements can be made to the conclusions as to which services the tuck shop could provide and what it should stock.

Stage 3 focuses on word-processing and desktop publishing software – producing formal letters to suppliers and prospective sponsors, creating posters and flyers or drawing up price lists, for example. If there are a large number of suppliers to be considered, a database may be set up and the letters produced via mail-merge. Figure 7.1 demonstrates some of the database fields that may be useful in this project.

To extend this part of the project, students with creative or artistic skills could create logos for the tuck shop which could be incorporated into their promotional material. The arts or media department could be approached to link in with this part of the project and a short study of brand logos could be conducted in readiness for the students to produce their own designs. This stage can still be carried out in small groups, with differentiation shown for skills and abilities where applicable.

Name of Company	Name of Contact	Telephone
Fruit Factory	Jacinta Smith	01208 123456
Mobile	Address #1	Address #2
07808 654321	3a Industrial Park	Belton
Address #3	Town/City	County
	Ringtown	Hampshire
	Postcode	
	RT5 6YE	

Website Address	Account Number
www.fruitybee.co.uk	SC1432-WDF
email address	Goods supplied
jacinta.smith@fruitybee.co.uk	Fresh fruit

Figure 7.1 Example of how the database might be constructed

At this point (stage 4) the students can be given either a theoretical budget, or a real budget if the tuck shop is really going to be opened (perhaps with local sponsorship if available). Discussions can include projected sales, setting up a rota for taking deliveries, when stocks should be replenished, how and when banking will occur, and so on. The budget will need to be included as part of a balance sheet (incorporating the use of spreadsheets) recording daily takings and expenditure (hopefully leading to a profit at the end of the term). There could be additional collaboration with the mathematics and business studies departments to ascertain the correct procedures for the preparation and presentation of a balance sheet. A stock control system can be set up as either a spreadsheet or database, depending on how much time is available and the abilities and skills of the students involved. It might be appropriate to offer differentiated activities to allow students to compare how various systems work within the project.

Stage 5 is the final stage before the tuck shop is ready to place orders with suppliers, stock the shelves and open its doors to customers. Advertising posters and flyers can now be distributed around the school, and to add a more exciting element to the project, audio and video advertising could be considered. For example, the students could **podcast** a radio-style advertisement and create video adverts which could be uploaded to YouTube, with students sending out links to the adverts in the same manner as they did for the survey at the commencement of the project.

With all of the preliminaries in place, the tuck shop is now ready to be launched, either theoretically or in reality (once a single model has been agreed upon between the different groups). The many stages of this project may have taken several weeks to complete, during which there will have been many opportunities to introduce a wide range of new materials or to reutilize existing skills in a new and more integrated way. There will have been opportunities to collaborate with other departments in the school to create a realistic feel to the project and further the idea that IT is not a standalone subject but rather a fully integrated subject. Elements of the project can be altered to suit the needs of the group, for example, the tuck shop can become a stationery shop, a uniform shop, a gift shop and so on. The amount of work the students are expected to do at each stage can be altered in accordance with available time and/or skill level. Elements of the project can be designed to fall in line with the requirements of whichever qualification is being taken. Chapter 5 indicates the range of qualifications at different levels.

Reflection 7.2

Does your establishment currently promote collaborative working across departments? Can you identify any opportunities?

Example project 2

This project is designed to be used with a class of adult beginners. There are many qualifications that adult learners may seek to enhance their career prospects. Chapter 5 has details of the different qualifications available at levels 1–3. There are also many adults who simply wish to acquire IT knowledge and have no desire for formal qualifications. Project-focused approaches involving relevant, meaningful topics can be much more useful (and interesting) to those seeking practical, non-accredited learning than traditional courses whose content can be largely irrelevant to them.

This project is concerned with an active retirement club. Such clubs vary in size from small groups of ex-colleagues and their partners to groups of hundreds of members; it is the latter type of group that should be the focus of the project as there is much more organization to be done. As with the first project, each component of the project can be reduced or extended to suit the needs of the class and their existing skills.

The retirement club can be described to students as either already being in existence or about to have their preliminary meeting. In either case, a form needs to be handed out to members requesting details such as full name, address, date of birth, telephone number and what their interests are. This personal information would be used for contact purposes and the information regarding their interests could be used to inform the social secretary of possible ideas when booking speakers, demonstrations, tours and day trips.

Stage 1 of the project is to design the form which will be used with the retirement club, and this can be done in class by dividing the students into pairs or groups of three and asking them to decide what should be included on the form. Once this has been agreed, the students can be introduced to setting out a simple form in a word-processing package. Examples are shown in Figures 7.2 and 7.3. If the existing skills of the students allow, this can be done as a table.

MEMBERSHIP FORM FOR RETIREMENT GROUP			
Name	Address		
Telephone		Mobile	
Email address			
Please tick if you would be interested in:	Attending talks	Day trips	Educational classes
	Fitness classes	Short breaks	Social gatherings
Please indicate your areas of general interest	Gardening	Photography	Crafts	Other, please specify:
	Family history	Sports	Dancing	

Figure 7.2 Example of a data capture form to be used with Project 2

MEMBERSHIP FORM FOR RETIREMENT GROUP

Please provide the following details:

Name ....
Address ....
....
Postcode ....
Telephone Number ....
Mobile Number ....
Email address..
Please tick if you would be interested in: Attending talks   ☐
                                            Day trips   ☐
                                            Educational classes   ☐
                                            Fitness classes   ☐
                                            Short breaks   ☐
                                            Social gatherings   ☐

Please indicate your areas of general interest: Gardening   ☐
                                                 Photography   ☐
                                                 Crafts   ☐
                                                 Family history   ☐
                                                 Sports   ☐
                                                 Dancing   ☐
                                                 Other, please specify
                                                 ....

Figure 7.3 Alternative example of a capture form to be used with Project 2

Stage 2 requires that several of these forms be completed by the students. Personal details should be fictitious in order to comply with the Data Protection Act. These data can then be used to create a database of members either in a spreadsheet or database application (once you have assessed the capabilities of your class). Discussions should be conducted within the group about the structure of the database and what it will be used for, as this will dictate the number of fields and their format, for example text field length. If using a database rather than a spreadsheet, consideration needs to be given to indices, primary key, uniqueness, and so on.

Once the template has been finalized, time should be allowed for students to enter the raw data into the database before anything further can be done. If you have confident learners, you may set this task to be completed out of class time once you have established their competence by entering a few records. Ideally there should be at least ten records to work with.

Stage 3 introduces many opportunities to bring in a variety of activities. From the initial forms, charts can be created to show the popularity of the different hobbies and interests using features of spreadsheet or database software. Students could plan advertising for a day trip or a future workshop session. The choice of whether to use a desktop publishing package or word-processing package will depend on time and student ability.

At stage 4, here the students can create a semi-formal letter to be mail-merged with the membership database to produce bulk mailings to all members. If the students' abilities are not yet sufficiently developed to undertake a mail-merge, labels can be set up in the word-processing package and have the names and addresses of members manually entered, ready to save for future use. The advertising created at stage 3, if this part of the project was done, could be included as part of this mailshot.

There are many ways in which this project can be altered to suit the needs of learners. With complete beginners it may be sufficient to design, type and discuss further uses of mailshots. The project could easily be adapted to suit a group of younger students; for example, for a group of 14–16-year-olds, the retirement club could become a youth group and the initial data form altered accordingly. The advertising part of the project would have similar content to Project 1 – using a video campaign and inviting members to events via links sent to social networking sites.

Reflection 7.3

Make a list of different self-contained lessons that you could usefully teach to a class of retirement-age students in a morning or afternoon. Consider their interests, needs and abilities in conjunction with what you expect their current skills base to be when doing this.

There are many self-contained lessons that can be designed for use with a group of older students to show how modern technologies can enhance their lives. Your list may have included some of the following:

Entertainment
- social networking
- booking theatre tickets
- renting DVDs
- watching missed television or radio programmes
- accessing television or radio programme website content
- downloading music/film/e-books (Chapter 3 has further details)
- entering competitions
- listening to live radio

Online shopping
- grocery shopping
- paying bills
- using price comparison sites find the best price for a given service or product
- ordering flowers
- buying gifts
- researching and booking holidays
- buying clothes
- arranging coach/train/airline tickets

Hobbies and interests
- researching information for hobbies
- researching family history
- accessing weather forecasts
- researching medical information
- route planning for car journeys
- accessing up-to-date traffic reports
- photo editing

Example project 3

This project is designed to be used with a group of small business owners and employees. There are still a surprising number of small businesses that use very little IT, but would like to be able to deploy it to enhance their accessibility to their customers.

This project is a way of demonstrating how different aspects of IT can enhance a company's business prospects and can simplify, modernize and streamline its day-to-day operation. Here we consider a fictitious business which is under threat of being taken over and modernized by a larger organization, unless it can reduce administrative overheads. The business can be any of your choosing, but here we will concentrate on a village 'alternative therapy' practice. The idea behind the project is that the employees of the business can gain insights into how IT could do this.

Stage 1 of this project requires the creation of a client database. As with the other projects, it is a good plan to split the class into small groups. The groups will brainstorm ideas to identify what the database will contain and need to be thinking about the nature of the different fields. It would also be good practice to discuss with your students how the database may be used in the future, for example to sort, query, mail-merge, produce reports and invoices and so on. This will help students to make better-informed decisions about what to include. They may decide to adapt an existing system or simply to design a new system from scratch.

Stage 2 focuses on creating promotional materials for the business and sending them out to clients. For example, the company may decide to run a 'five treatments for the price of four' offer. Word-processing or desktop publishing software can be used to create flyers that can then be included with other correspondence from the business to its clients. Whether or not each client receives mail-merged correspondence will depend upon the correct fields having been set in the database (allowing clients to opt out of mailings). The mail-merge lesson is an excellent time to include examples of how databases can be created which are difficult to use for mail-merging even though all of the relevant information is present (for example, single-line rather than multi-line addresses, names entered as 'surname', 'forename' fields).

Stage 3 requires the groups to set up a simple spreadsheet in which to detail their daily income and expenditure, similar to a manual daybook. Simple formulae can be taught as well as linking one page of a spreadsheet to another, facilitating easy or automatic updating of the saved spreadsheet at a later time. Students can be shown how to add additional pages to a spreadsheet and to move and rename them for different months of the year. Whilst these are only small features, they demonstrate how IT can make businesses users more efficient.

Stage 4 demonstrates the power of the internet and communication via e-mail. It is likely that the students' suppliers provide on-line ordering services via their websites, and the ability to use such services is likely to make ordering more efficient and cost-effective, reducing the need to store large amounts of stock. If the students' business can be contacted via e-mail, clients will be able to book appointments online, making for a more flexible system better aligned with modern lifestyles.

If any of the students become especially interested in the application of IT, they could learn to create their own website for their business.

Stage 5 involves teaching students how to use personal organizer software, for example Microsoft **Outlook** or Lotus Notes, in order to manage an appointments diary. It is possible to export or link the clients' details from the database into the personal organizer software to eliminate the need for duplicate manual entry. Eventually, the diary part of the personal organizer could be linked up to the business website so that customers can modify their own details, book their own appointment times from those shown as available, request additional details on treatments and so on.

The project as outlined could apply to a large range of small businesses in need of IT such as a craft shop, small garage, sports injury clinic, private tutor, florist, photographic studio and so on. Any element of the project can be taught as a standalone lesson or just a couple of the elements could be combined to make a 10-hour course. There is scope for further discussion so that students can gain an understanding of how other technologies may be of use to them at a later date. There is also flexibility within the project to structure it into two or three short courses which the students could choose to attend as and when their requirements and commitments allowed.

Summary of Key Points

- Project-based learning using blended strategies can motivate learners to extend their repertoire of knowledge and link learning directly to the workplace.
- Projects are adaptable to incorporate the interests, learning styles and abilities of a wide range of students.
- Teaching strategies can promote cross-curricular learning at a variety of different levels.
- Larger projects can be divided into smaller elements to provide more flexible approaches.

Useful websites

http://www.surveymonkey.com
http://www.facebook.com
http://www.twitter.com
http://www.myspace.com
http://www.bebo.com
http://www.openoffice.com
http://www.freeonlinesurveys.com
http://freemind.sourceforge.net
http://www.youtube.com
http://www.bolt.com
http://www.blogster.com
http://www.myopera.com
http://dailybooth.com
http://www.mypodcast.com
http://audacity.download-latest.com

Further reading

Abram, C. and Pearlman, L. (2008) *Facebook for Dummies*. Indianapolis: Wiley.
Clarke, A. (2008) *E-learning Skills*, 2nd edn. Basingstoke: Palgrave Macmillan.
Fitton, L., Gruen, M. and Poston, L. (2009) *Twitter for Dummies*. Indianapolis: Wiley.

8

Assessment

In this chapter we will focus on:

- The purpose of assessment.
- Planning for assessment in IT, including initial and diagnostic assessment, **ipsative** and self-assessment, formative and summative strategies.
- Formative assessment strategies and the importance of assessment for learning.
- Reliability, validity and sufficiency in IT assessments.
- Authenticity and strategies for assessing group and collaborative working in IT projects.
- Planning and preparing for e-assessment.
- Planning for supportive and inclusive assessment, including blended assessment methodologies and differentiated assessments.
- Summative assessment and the importance of assessment of learning in IT.

What is assessment?

Assessment in education is concerned with evidencing how much learning has taken place. It incorporates a multitude of judgements by teachers, examiners, observers and mentors and has many stakeholders, among them government departments, funding agencies, employers, senior managers in educational establishments, examination boards, curriculum planners, administrative personnel, teachers and, of course, crucially, the students themselves.

Tummons (2007, p. 4) defines assessment as a means of testing to 'discover whether or not the learner could perform a specified task in a workshop, or to judge the extent to which the learner has mastered a new skill or a new body of theoretical knowledge'.

Assessment is most readily thought of as a process that leads directly to the awarding of a qualification through summative testing such as an examination, though this does not necessarily have to be the case. Initial, diagnostic and formative forms of assessment also play vital roles in student achievement and are essential in motivating and encouraging learners through differentiated learning and teaching practices.

Initial assessment

In IT, as in any subject, the purpose of initial assessment is to identify, for example, the additional support needs of students, motivation and confidence levels, the student's reasons for selecting the course, levels of study skills, and what interests a student may have outside the programme, so that learning can be appropriately contextualized and an individual learning plan (**ILP**) can be created. On IT courses it is essential to determine whether students have access to similar computer programs and hardware in their homes and at their place of learning as this will affect their ability to complete homework and practice between lessons. In many adult and community courses initial assessment usually takes place over the first few weeks. In other educational establishments such as schools and colleges, with their larger class numbers, this process may take a little longer. This information is likely to be gained through tutorials and group debate.

Diagnostic assessment

During the initial assessment phase it is also vital to determine how much a student already understands in terms of IT and whether that knowledge is practical or theoretical. For adults undertaking a beginners' class, it may be that all the learners will be starting from the same level of knowledge, but those engaged in more advanced classes and younger 'digital natives' are much more likely to have very 'spiky' profiles, as discussed in Chapter 6.

Diagnostic assessment is a process that identifies a learner's current levels of IT functional skills, information literacy and media literacy and compares them to those required by the examination or course syllabus. There is, after all, nothing more demoralizing for a student than to repeat areas that they are already fully conversant with. The results of diagnostic assessment also feed into the ILP and aid the teacher in determining how they will approach the teaching, what teaching and learning strategies they will employ and how they will assess future learning. Figure 8.1 summarizes the diagnostic and initial assessment process.

For students who have at least some knowledge, an IT method of gaining contributions to diagnostic assessment information is to set students an IT task. It would be impossible to determine the starting point of every student for every part of the IT course at the beginning of the programme, and so diagnostic testing is repeated at the beginning of each new section of learning, for example, at the beginning of a new module or unit. Diagnostic assessment can also be useful to undertake both during and at the end of each part of the same section of learning to identify progress that each student has made against their own individual initial benchmark both during their studies and in preparation for a final, summative examination.

Mind-mapping software and surveys are resources that can be used both diagnostically and as a teaching and learning resource, as discussed in Chapter 7.

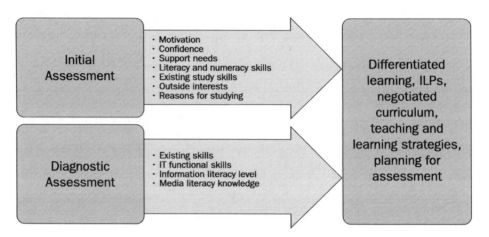

Figure 8.1 Initial and diagnostic assessment

Examples of diagnostic assessments

Examples of implementing diagnostic assessments are ipsative/self-assessment questionnaires, online quizzes, practical skills application and mind-maps, which is perhaps a more innovative method.

Paper-based self-assessment (ipsative) questionnaires can be devised by the teacher to start the process of recognizing current skills. They are useful because a student can return to their questionnaire at any stage of the course to compare their progress, annotating the various questions and dating their responses. However, as with all self-assessments, they are not always an accurate benchmark of a learner's current abilities as the terminology used may not be understood or students may over- or under-score their skills.

Online tests covering the unit or course criteria are often available from institutions such as E-Skills UK (http://www.e-skills.com) or can be created by the teacher using survey software. Survey Monkey is free-to-download software (http://www.surveymonkey.com) and teachers can use the lesson outcomes as a basis for the questions. Online tests are particularly suitable for IT students as skills such as mouse manipulation and keyboard skills can also be observed by the teacher if they are conducted during study time. They can also be readily e-mailed and the results can be analysed automatically.

Practical activities can be a fun and interesting way of determining skill and confidence level kinaesthetically and encourage the students to get involved. This activity can also be used as an icebreaker if students are grouped together. Some ideas for the activities are: composing a letter and e-mailing it, devising a simple software routine, scanning an image, taking and downloading a digital image and creating a digital soundbite. Where equipment is scarce a 'circuit' activity can be devised where students partake in all these activities in turn and move around the room in groups to 'visit' the next activity.

Mind-maps can be used creatively to allow students to explore their IT skills visually. Students can create electronic or paper-based mind-maps, either individually or collaboratively, to indicate what is already known about a topic. If working individually, students can then either use the software or coloured pens to assign a colour to specific areas of the map to indicate how proficient or confident they feel about the various aspects noted. For example, green could be used to signify proficiency, red to denote where a concept is new or untried, and orange to indicate a new skill that needs more practice. These maps can be revisited later and extended as new skills are developed, and the colours can be updated to give a visual representation of progress. Mind-maps also help some students with their study skills, and this is an excellent opportunity to introduce them as a way of visually representing abstract concepts. A free-to-download version of an i-map is available at http://freemind.sourceforge.net or you could use any mind-mapping software, or use an electronic whiteboard to capture and distribute mind-maps.

Formative assessment

Formative assessment occurs throughout the learning process, aiding both student and teacher to check that the teaching has been understood. As with other subjects, formative assessments in IT can be either formal or informal, assessing cognitive process skills, practical skills or 'soft' skills such as confidence in using IT.

The main purpose of formative assessment is for a teacher to be able to give constructive feedback to learners (and often other stakeholders) on their progress, and, very importantly, for students to have their say about what they have learnt. This two-way feedback is essential in establishing and maintaining motivation. However, this is only part of the story. According to the assessment for learning reforms (Assessment Reform Group 2002) formative assessment information should be fed back into the planning cycle to help teachers and learners to plan for the next steps in the learning process through feedback and by updating the ILP. This is known as assessment *for* learning rather than assessment *of* learning, which is more associated with the summative assessment process. In summary, the reforms state that students improve most if they know:

- why they are learning;
- where they are now along the learning path;
- where they need to go next;
- and how best to get there.

Feedback can come from a variety of sources, including teachers, peers, and colleagues, and from students reviewing their own learning, and can be in either written or verbal form. In group assessments students can compare their learning with that of others, and feedback from other students can, while not being as authoritative, be very valuable. One way of eliciting feedback from a learner about their own assessment is to ask:

- What did you do best/least well in this assessment, and why?

- What was the most difficult part of this assignment, and why?
- What did you enjoy the most about this assignment, and why?
- What do you consider to be the most important thing you learned and why?

For peer assessments the questions can be slightly rephrased:

- What do you think the learner did best/least well in this assessment, and why?
- What did you enjoy the most about this assignment, and why?
- What did you learn from the presentation and how will it affect your own learning?

The responses to such questions should feed back into the overall formative assessment process, helping the teacher to identify how to proceed and the learner to review what they have learnt and what they need to concentrate on next. Figure 8.2 indicates this formative assessment process.

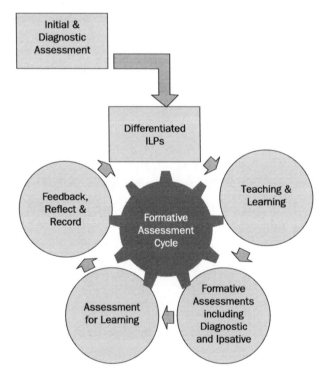

Figure 8.2 Relationships between initial, diagnostic and formative assessments

Formative assessment strategies

Formative assessments come in many guises, such as questions and answers, discussions, group presentations, project work, coursework, and independent research. In IT assessments it is very likely that IT will also be used as the main vehicle for gathering, presenting and evidencing learning. However, we believe that a blended approach to formative assessment, using elements from other curricula such as role play and discussions, works equally well in IT.

We often observe the printing of repetitious and uninteresting screen dumps to evidence incremental steps in the building of, for example, websites, and this is often justified by the need to evidence process skills, rather like showing workings-out in mathematics. However, in informal formative assessments cognitive information can be extrapolated from the end product and by allowing the teacher to make professional judgements. Any formal formative assessment needs to reflect a balance of practical tests, appropriate capturing of soft skills and the inclusion of questions that test higher, medium and lower cognitive knowledge. In addition, assessments should be reliable, valid, sufficient and authentic.

Reliability

Reliability in assessment ensures that different assessors would consistently award identical marks for the same piece of work by a student. A high level of reliability is best obtained when assessment criteria are objective and where any subjective personal views are minimized. Much of the IT curriculum lends itself to the easy creation of objective assessment criteria, for example: 'A student will be able to cut and copy and paste a specified paragraph within the same word processed document and between two different word processed documents'. Objective criteria ensure that the assessment of whether a student can or cannot do something is clear and therefore reliability is built into the assessment from the start.

Subjective or 'soft' outcomes are more difficult, if not impossible, to measure reliably, and different assessors may award different marks accordingly. For example: 'A student will be able to discuss different hardware options with a client with confidence'. This learning criterion is open to interpretation and requires a teacher to make judgements based on their own professional abilities.

Case Study 8.1

A teacher wishes to assess whether her students have understood the use of the phrase 'IT peripheral'. She has drafted several questions as follows:

Q1. Tick three of the following which are not peripheral devices.

    Printer   Mouse   Laptop
    Hardware Keyboard Software

Q2. Name three computer peripheral devices.

Q3. Name three computer peripheral devices and describe their functions.

Q4. Name at least three computer peripherals and explain in detail their function, some common faults that may occur with them and how to fix such faults.

Q5. Choose three peripheral devices from the range of computer equipment provided and demonstrate the correct procedure for connecting them to the computer provided.

Reflection 8.1

Which questions are more likely to provide reliable assessments? Which are most likely to test higher cognitive (problem solving) skills and why?

The most reliable are those that will have only one interpretation, so Q1, Q2 and Q5 are most reliable as they do not require any description that will be open to subjective interpretation. Q5 asks the student to demonstrate their practical skills so they will not only have to select peripheral devices from a range of hardware, but also have to recognize what they look like and how they can be connected in real-life situations. Q4 and Q5 provide the most opportunity for a student to display higher levels of cognition.

Reflection 8.2

Review your assessment methods. How do you ensure reliability?

Validity

Assessments should also be valid. Validity ensures that the assessment method chosen matches the learning objectives and that it tests what it is meant to test. For example, a teacher should assess students on how they would input data into a database by asking them to demonstrate how they would type data into appropriate fields and not by asking them to write an essay on the subject. The latter tests a student's ability to describe what is required, and their level of literacy skills will become part of the success, or otherwise, of the assessment. It is also essential that the results of the assessment are useful in either allowing constructive feedback to be given to the learner in formative activities or that a summative assessment leading to the awarding of a qualification is an appropriate benchmark for the learner to take into the workplace.

Case Study 8.2

A group of learners have come to the end of a lesson on the computer hardware that makes up a computer base station. Diagrams and a vocabulary sheet have been provided during the teaching to remind students about the constituent parts of a computer along with a list of the units of measurement associated with random access memory (**RAM**), processor speed and hard disk size. The teaching also included a video demonstrating how a hardware technician upgraded the RAM on a PC. As a formative assessment the teacher asked the students to label the positions of the central processing unit (**CPU**), RAM slots, video slot, **PCI** expansion slots and USB ports on Figure 8.3.

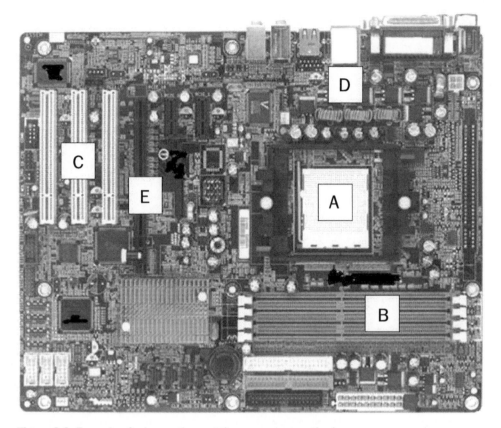

Figure 8.3 Example of a 'name the parts' assessment method

Reflection 8.3

How reliable and valid is this assessment method?

We would suggest that this assessment is reliable: two different teachers would be very likely to award the same marks as the student diagrams indicating the various parts would be easy to evidence. It also tests knowledge of some computer hardware, but we would argue that it is insufficient to test more cognitive processes such as problem-solving. Furthermore, it is not a valid form of assessment if the student will be required to perform a chip change in the summative examination rather than writing about it or for purchasing a PC in a computer store as it is unlikely that the student would be able to discuss technical aspects such as processor speed and RAM size with a supplier to any great extent.

Reflection 8.4

Review your assessment methods. How do you ensure validity?

Sufficiency

This aspect of assessment refers to what Saunders and Race (1992) term 'shades of competency'. The question to ask is: how many times and to what depth does a learner need to evidence something before they can be said to be sufficiently competent at it? During formative assessment, sufficiency is achieved by reassessing skills over a period of time, but in summative assessment the student is usually only given a single attempt.

Reflection 8.5

Return to Case Study 8.2. How confident are you that success in this formative assessment would be sufficient to allow a student to upgrade the RAM in their own PC? How would you devise a more appropriate form of assessment for this learning objective?

The more personally a student is involved with their learning the more likely they are to internalize and perform well in assessments and in real-life situations (Pask 1975). Asking a student to physically take a computer apart (many institutions are littered with non-functioning or older models) is often very daunting, and particularly adult students have an almost tangible fear of opening a computer to see what is inside. However, tactile and visual formative assessment based on a real-life approach can effect enormous changes in the way that students of all ages think about computers. Asking students to physically plug and unplug a chip set onto a motherboard will create long-term learning to be embedded much more than if the teacher simply talks about it conceptually. It also makes the sufficiency of the assessment easier to assess.

An alternative might be to offer students a fictitious budget and ask them to design their own computer with appropriate CPU, RAM, network cards, wireless cards, USB ports and so on. This allows for research on which components would be most appropriate, how much they would cost and where the parts could be sourced from.

Reflection 8.6

Review your assessment methods. How do you ensure sufficiency?

Authenticity

Group assessment strategies in IT are valuable because they mirror the team work that students will use in their careers and they help to develop social skills and confidence.

However, group assessment also adds an extra difficulty to the assessment process for a teacher. The question becomes centred on the students' respective contributions to the assessment process, and only the members of the group will ever really know who has participated and to what level. Indeed, this is an inherent difficulty with any group presentation or collaborative project-based assessment.

Any work, including coursework, homework, distance learning and e-learning, that is not completed in a supervised learning environment is open to the challenge that the student may have collaborated with others during the process and that the work produced is therefore not entirely their own.

Case Study 8.3

You have asked a group to put together a presentation on a project about selecting and purchasing a mobile phone. There are four students in each group, and you have provided them with a project brief that lists examples of who the client might be, how much money they have to spend and what they may wish to use the mobile phone for. The groups report back in a variety of ways:

- Two members of group 1 present research findings by way of a Microsoft **Power-Point** presentation and have brought in some ex-demonstration models that they have borrowed from a local mobile phone company to show the different styles available.
- Group 2 present their project through the use of a video that they have subsequently uploaded to YouTube, showing members of their group interviewing different 'clients' and providing a handout for the other students on the advantages and disadvantages of six different mobile phones, including costs.
- Group 3 present their findings verbally. Each member of the group speaks in turn on the part of the research they have been involved in, and they provide a list of web addresses they have researched.
- Group 4 present their examples of e-mail correspondence with manufacturers and a Facebook discussion on suggestions for appropriate mobile phones. They have also produced a booklet showing their research.

Reflection 8.7

How would you go about assessing these very diverse group presentations, and how would you determine a mark for each individual student?

There are no quick-fix solutions to such issues of authenticity, but Race (2000) suggests the following range of approaches:

- **Use the same group mark for all involved**. This can be viewed by students as unfair, and only assesses the final product and not the inherent processes that have contributed to it.

- **Divide the assessment between the group members from the beginning**. It can be difficult to divide tasks equally, though it will be easier to recognize the contributions of individuals in this way. This approach will also increase the assessment overhead for teachers.

- **Award an overall mark and then allow students to distribute them**. The teacher marks the final group presentation, for example 300 out of a possible 400 marks (= 4 group members × 100), and then allows the students in the group to decide how those 300 marks should be allocated between them. This assessment strategy is seen as fair, but peer-assessment requires an emotionally mature group of students to reach a fair consensus.

- **Award the same mark and then test individuals separately**. Here all the students in the group are given the same mark based on the assessment product. Then the teacher sets either a verbal or written assessment to ascertain how much individual knowledge has been learnt, but this is different from how much a student has contributed to the task. Although this process allows individuals to receive additional marks, formal tests of this nature may reduce validity of the assessment as some members may find it more difficult to explain themselves verbally or the teacher may test for outcomes that they were not involved in. It will also involve a great deal of preparation by the teacher.

E-assessment

Many IT assessments lend themselves to the use of e-assessment methodologies, for example, **e-portfolios**, online tests, blogs, podcasts, **wikis**, VLEs and discussion boards. Such methodologies offer reliable assessments with rapid turnaround of marking for feedback to students, but questions are restricted to those such as multiple-choice, numerical, true/false, gap-fill and matching pairs. Essay questions still require human assessment, but can be sent, marked and returned electronically (saving time, money and paper) and the teacher can automatically keep a record of any progress and achievement. Many VLEs have the equivalent of a grade book where students can log on to collect and comment on their feedback and grades, and some schools are beginning to adopt this method as a means of communicating with parents and guardians on a student's progress. Many adult IT courses such as CLAiT, ECDL and ITQ routinely incorporate online computer-based assessments as part of their assessment strategies, and these are increasingly being used in schools, colleges and higher education. When e-assessment goes according to plan it is cost-effective and efficient. However, there are inherent issues with e-assessment that also need to be carefully considered, for example:

- **Hardware and software failure**. The test centre will need to ensure there are additional computer workstations and duplicate printers available in the examination room.

- **Power loss**. Paper copies of the e-assessment will need to be available in case of widespread power failure and also robust back-up procedures will be needed to automatically save assessments as they are completed.

- **Security**. Assessments and answer files need to be kept secure, preferably on a closed internal network. Procedures also need to be in place in case of data corruption. Computer log-ins and passwords will need to be prepared in advance. If students are allowed to bring material in to the assessment on portable devices such as pen drives, these will need to be checked for viruses and disallowed data before they can be used.

- **Environmental preparation**. The IT teacher and/or an IT technician will need to supervise the computer environment to run systems tests prior to the students' arrival, check hardware and ensure that the computers are suitably spaced to minimize the risks of students viewing other screens.

- **Advance preparation**. Teachers will need to prepare students for the assessments in advance so they are comfortable with different types of responses and how to correct mistakes. After all, assessments should test content and not a student's ability to navigate the examination system. Students will also need written and verbal instructions on how to log on, passwords and where to save, print and back up files.

The outcomes of IT courses easily lend themselves to the creation of e-portfolios that gather together electronic assessments such as projects, evidence of learning including video clips, podcasts, photographs and written work, and formative feedback from teachers, peers and the students themselves. It is a green and convenient method of storing and sharing information with assessors and awarding bodies, though secure back-up procedures must be maintained to reduce the possibility of data loss.

Planning for assessment

Just as poor planning can lead to poor learning and teaching, poor assessment planning can lead to confusing and difficult assessments. Assessment should be considered and integrated into lesson planning as much as a teacher plans resources and timings. The following steps indicate how this may be achieved:

- Consider the syllabus and scheme of work.
- Check cut-off dates for coursework, exam entries and examination dates.
- Ensure that any student requiring specialist or assistive technology and IT equipment is accommodated and allow time for the student to practise beforehand if the technology or equipment is unfamiliar to them.
- Contact the examination boards as soon as possible to arrange for additional examination time or to gain agreement for an amanuensis (note-taker) or for verbal or written instructions to be provided.
- Always add contingency time into the timetable in case students are unable to attend formative assessments or in case IT equipment fails.
- Are all students going to be examined simultaneously or will they sit assessments when they are ready, for example, ECDL, ITQ and CLAiT courses?

Brown and Glasner (1999) note that in a typical UK degree course, written examinations and tutor-marked assignments dominate assessment planning, accounting for approximately 90 per cent of the assessments.

However, this narrow range of assessment and feedback strategies should be broadened and based on an integrative approach which balances the elements of assessment for learning with accessibility, diversity, economy and achievement. This raises the idea of 'blended assessments' that are not necessarily based on the use of IT to assess IT. These non-IT assessments may be more appropriate for assessing 'soft skills' such as communication, listening and confidence.

Inclusive assessment

Equality and inclusivity in assessment are maintained through rigorous checking of the consistency and quality of activities. Well-planned assessments should be differentiated in order to ensure that there is no advantage for one learner over another and that suitable arrangements are made for inclusive assessment in terms of any assistive technology and additional time, as discussed earlier in this chapter. Assessments still need to remain valid, reliable, authentic and sufficient.

In formative assessments teachers can set differentiated questions for learners based on their abilities, in order to challenge everyone in the class without over-challenging and demotivating those with limited knowledge, while still challenging and motivating those with more ability in a subject. An example of how this can be achieved is given below.

> **Reflection 8.8**
>
> Refer to the question in Case Study 8.2. How could this question be altered very simply to test different levels? How would the changes affect validity and reliability?

The answer to this lies in the amount of assistance given to the student. As it stands, the question has already given the names of the hardware and the labels indicate where these items are on the motherboard. Essentially this is a matching exercise, requesting the learner to pair up the letters on the diagram to the corresponding list of responses given. Alternatives in increasing order of difficulty are as follows:

- **Simply remove the labels from the diagram**. In this way the student has to know what a CPU looks like from a whole range of hardware rather than from a selection of five.

- **Remove not only the labels, but also the list of hardware parts** to be named from the question. Ask the student to select, label and name five parts of a motherboard. In this way the student has to know the names of five parts on a motherboard and know what they look like without any prompts.

- **Add a supplementary question** which might ask learners not only to locate and label five parts of the motherboard, but also to accurately describe their function and any units of measurement associated with them.

This final question would test higher cognitive levels and be a valid form of assessment. However, unlike the original question, it could not be marked by a computer and so marking and feedback may take more time and be more complex. Reliability depends on the accurate interpretation of the answer by a teacher.

This illustrates the balance that is needed in setting assessments. Concern over the use of multiple-choice questions is often expressed, especially with regard to evidencing deeper analysis and synthesis of knowledge. For this reason a well-planned formal assessment will contain a variety of blended question types, including:

- multiple choice
- matching pairs
- short responses
- long responses
- practical demonstrations.

In addition, formal assessments in IT may also include:

- coursework and portfolio building, including witness statements from work placements, photographs and written assignments. E-portfolios may also include evidence through wikis, blogs, digital photographs, podcasts, video clips, presentations and so on.

Formative assessment strategies should be as varied as those used in teaching and learning to ensure that learners are actively engaged and motivated in their learning. Good formative assessment design should form an integral part of the planning process. Aiding students to recognize their own progression through differentiated assessment strategies fosters inclusivity. Such practices can support and guide students towards becoming more autonomous learners.

However, although IT has many positive qualities that can assist learners to overcome barriers to assessment and facilitate their attainment of qualifications, it is the responsibility of the teacher to ensure that the questions check for IT skills and are not reliant on inappropriate levels of language or a learner being able to access appropriate hardware and software at home.

Summative assessment

Summative assessment occurs at the end of a course or section of learning, for example at the end of a unit or module. Rather than assessment *for* learning, summative activities are concerned with assessment *of* learning. Examination boards will set questions that test lower, intermediate and higher cognitive levels, using a variety of question types like those listed above, and so students should be familiar with the

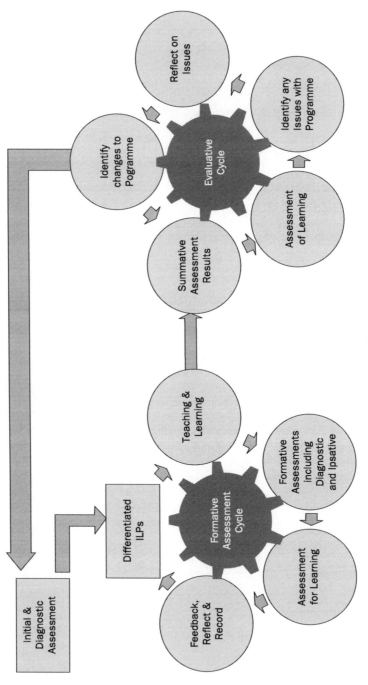

Figure 8.4 The role of assessment in the evaluative cycle

assessment strategy. It is also the responsibility of the teacher to ensure that inclusivity is planned for, as explained earlier in this chapter.

In reality the boundaries between formative and summative assessments are often blurred, especially when assessing through continuous processes such as portfolio building and coursework. It must, however, be recognized that formative assessment allows a learner to submit a piece of work that they can later modify on the basis of feedback. In summative assessments, the student has no such opportunity.

Some IT examinations, such as ECDL and CLAiT modules, can be taken when an individual student is ready to take them, without having to wait for the whole group. Pedagogically this is very motivating for students, but increased administrative support will be needed to ensure that examination protocols are maintained and that suitable venues and invigilation can be arranged.

Summative assessment results should always feed back into the evaluative cycle of the programme, module or course so that examination results are included in the overall evaluation of the success of a course, as demonstrated in Figure 8.4. Changes to the course should be incorporated and planned for in the initial and diagnostic stages of any subsequent programmes.

Summary of Key Points

- Planning is critical to ensure inclusive, interesting and motivating formative assessment activities.
- Formative assessment strategies are vital in developing assessment for learning strategies that will motivate students by guiding them through their learning.
- Any assessment should be tested for reliability, validity, equality and sufficiency.
- Group and collaborative assessments do not have to be onerous. This teaching method can add value to learning by encouraging self- and peer assessment.
- Assessment has a crucial role to play in ensuring curriculum quality.

Further reading

Clarke, A. (2008) *E-learning Skills*, 2nd edn. Basingstoke: Palgrave Macmillan.

Glossary

Amazon	Online store specializing in books, music, electronic goods and others (http://www.amazon.com, http://www.amazon.co.uk)
AQA	Assessment and Qualifications Alliance, a nationally recognized examination and awarding body (http://www.aqa.org.uk)
AS	Advanced Subsidiary level, a nationally recognized level of qualification
ASCENTIS	A nationally recognized examination group and awarding body (http://www.ascentis.co.uk)
ASCILITE	A nationally recognized examination group and awarding body (http://www.ascilite.org.au)
ASDAN	Award Scheme Development and Accreditation Network, a nationally recognized examination group and awarding body (http://www.asdan.org.uk/)
Assistive technology	Adaptive equipment for supporting disabled students
AUP	Acceptable Use Policy, an organization's internal policy for acceptable or permitted use of IT equipment
Avatar	A graphical image representing a person (typically on the internet)
Back-up	Files copied to safeguard files from loss or corruption
BBC	British Broadcasting Corporation
BCS	British Computer Society (http://www.bcs.org/)
Bebo	Bebo ('Blog Early, Blog Often') is a social networking site (http://www.bebo.com)
BeBook	A lightweight, handheld e-book reader (models include BeBook One, BeBook Neo, BeBook Mini (http://www.mybebook.com)
BERA	British Educational Research Association
BETT	British Educational Training and Technology, synonymous with a large annual educational technology event
BIS	Department of Business Innovation and Skills
BlackBerry	Wireless mobile device produced by Research In Motion, incorporating

	smart phone applications and telephone functionality (http://www.rim.com)
Blended learning	A mix of technological and non-IT learning strategies and resources
Blog	Abbreviation of web-log. Websites containing personal materials typically including news about an individual's activities
BTEC	Businesses and Technology Council
CCEA	Council for the Curriculum Examinations and Assessment, a nationally recognized examination group and awarding body (http://www.ccea.org.uk/)
CCIE	Cisco Certified Internetwork Expert, an IT professional certification on Cisco Systems products
CCNA	Cisco Certified Network Associate, an IT professional certification on Cisco Systems products
CCNP	Cisco Certified Network Professional, an IT professional certification on Cisco Systems products
CCTV	Closed-Circuit Television, a system of security cameras
CD	Compact Disc
Channel 4oD	Channel 4 on Demand–, an application provided by Channel 4 TV allowing users to watch programmes they have missed online (http://www.channel4.com/programmes/4od)
CIE	University of Cambridge International Examinations, a nationally recognized examination and awarding body (http://www.cie.org.uk/)
Cisco	A leading manufacturer of networking equipment (http://www.cisco.com)
CITP	Chartered IT Professional
City and Guilds	The City and Guilds of London Institute, a nationally recognized examination and awarding body
CLAiT	Computer Literacy and Information Technology level 1 qualification
CLAiT PLUS	The OCR level 2 Certificate for IT Users
COBOL	COmmon Business-Oriented Language, one of the oldest programming languages (*c.* 1960)
Collaborative projects	Learning in co-operation with other students via the completion of projects
CPD	Continuing Professional Development
CPU	Central Processing Unit, the hardware component which executes software instructions
DCSF	Department for Children, Schools and Families
DfEE	Department for Education and Employment
Downloading	Transferring files and data from an external source
DVD	Digital Video Disc
eBay	Online auction site (http://www.ebay.com)
ECDL	European Computer Driving Licence

EdExcel	A nationally recognized examination and awarding body, part of Pearson (http://www.edexcel.com)
EDI	Education Development International, an accredited awarding body and leading international education company (http://www.ediplc.com/)
E-assessment	Assessment that is collected and returned through IT
E-book	An electronic book is one that is held and viewed in electronic form
E-green	Guidelines for reducing environmental impact through the use of technology
E-learning	Learning that is delivered through the medium of IT
E-mail	Electronic mail
E-portfolio	An electronic means of storing and retrieving assessed material and research
E-reader	A device on which to read e-books
E-safety	Guidelines for responsible internet use
E-Skills UK	An organization focused on improving and promoting UK IT skills (http://www.e-skills.com)
Facebook	Social networking site (http://www.facebook.com)
Fax	Abbreviation for 'facsimile'. Fax machines send copies of documents between remote sites using the telephone network. Now largely superseded by e-mail (and attachments)
Firewall	Security system to protect technology and data from unauthorized access
FON	Free Open Network, a BT facility to give others the opportunity to share unused bandwidth
Freecycle	An international community promoting the reuse and sharing of goods which would otherwise end up as refuse (http://www.uk.freecycle.org)
Gantt chart	A horizontal bar chart showing event sequences and dependencies
GCE	General Certificate of Education
GCSE	General Certificate of Secondary Education
GLH	Guided Learning Hours
Gmail	Google's e-mail service
Google	One of the most popular search engines (http://www.google.com)
Google Books	Electronic book service provided by Google
HAAS	Hardware As A Service
HSE	Health and Safety Executive
HTTP	Hypertext Transfer Protocol
HTTPS	Hypertext Transfer Protocol over Secure Socket Layer, a secure protocol designed to be used in conjunction with HTTP on websites where there is the need for encryption of data (see also SSL)
Hypermedia	Graphics, text, audio and hyperlinks combined together to create a non-linear medium of information
IBM	International Business Machines, a leading manufacturer of hardware and software

ICAA	International Curriculum and Assessment Agency (http://www.icaa.com)
ICAAE	International Curriculum and Assessment Agency Examination
ICT	Information and Communications Technologies
IGCSE	International GCSE, an international curriculum and qualification for 14–16-year-olds
ILP	Individual Learning Plan
ILT	Information Learning Technologies
IM	Instant Messaging
Interflora	A worldwide grouping of florists distributing flowers and gifts under a collective banner (http://www.interflora.com)
Internet	The global system of interconnected computer networks
Intranet	Internal network that helps to keep information secure within a company or educational establishment
iPhone	A smartphone produced by Apple Inc. combining telephone, internet access, WiFi connectivity, camera, etc.
iPlayer	BBC iPlayer allows users to download and view missed television programmes
Ipsative	Reiterative self-assessment
ISP	Internet Service Provider
IT	Information Technology
ITQ	Information Technology Qualification
iTunes	Apple Inc's digital media player application. iTunes Store is an online store where users can download music
jetBook	An e-book reader supporting a wide range of e-book formats (http://www.jetbook.net)
Kazaa	Peer-to-peer file sharing application
LLiDA	Learning Literacies for a Digital Age, a short study into learning literacies in UK higher and further education
LLUK	Lifelong Learning UK
LSIS	Lifelong Learning and Skills Improvement Service
MCA	Microsoft Certified Architect, an IT professional certification for Microsoft products
MCAD	Microsoft Certified Application Developer, an IT professional certification for Microsoft products
MCSA	Microsoft Certified Systems Administrator, an IT professional certification for Microsoft products
MCSD	Microsoft Certified Solution Developer, an IT professional certification for Microsoft products
MCSE	Microsoft Certified Systems Engineer, an IT professional certification for Microsoft products
MFD	Multi-Function Device, a device with more than one use. For example, a peripheral which can function as a fax, scanner, copier and printer

Microsoft Windows	An operating system designed for PCs and PC networks
Mind-map	A form of diagram used to organize thoughts, tasks and ideas
Mirroring	Automatic duplicating method of real-time file storage
MP3	A digital system for encoding voice and video data to be played on an MP3 player, on a mobile phone, computer, etc.
Napster	An online music file sharing service (closed by court order in 2001), spawning a number of similar services
NCFE	Northern Council for Further Education
NIACE	National Institute of Adult Continuing Education
NOCN	National Open College Network (www.nocn.org.uk)
NVQ	National Vocational Qualification
OCR	Oxford Cambridge and RSA Examinations (www.ocr.org.uk)
OneNote	Microsoft OneNote is a package for multi-user collaboration and free-form information gathering and collation
Outlook	Microsoft Outlook is an e-mail client and personal information management application (contacts, calendar, etc.)
Palm Pilot	An early make of PDA popular before the advent of the smartphone
PayPal	PayPal is a subsidiary of eBay providing safe, secure online shopping without the need to provide suppliers with credit card details
PC	Personal Computer
PDA	Personal Digital Assistant
Phishing	Fraudulent activity aimed at acquiring usernames, passwords, credit card details, etc.
PIN	Personal Identification Number
Podcast	An audio file that can be downloaded for listening later
PowerPoint	A Microsoft Office application allowing creation of professional presentations and associated materials
Psion	The Psion Organiser was an early PDA popular before the advent of the smartphone
RAM	Random Access Memory
SAAS	Software As A Service
Skype	Free-to-download software for routeing voice calls over the internet
Sky Player	An application provided by Sky TV allowing their customers to watch programmes they have missed on-line (http://skyplayer.sky.com)
Spam	Unwanted e-mail communications
SQA	Scottish Qualifications Authority
SSAT	Special Schools and Academies Trust
Twitter	A social networking site commonly used for blogging
uBid	On-line auction site (http://www.ubid.com)
Uploading	Transferring files and data to an external site
USB	Universal Serial Bus

VDU	Visual Display Unit – computer monitor
Virtualization	The abstraction of computer resources allowing multiple virtual computers to be created on a single physical machine
Virus	Unsolicited and potentially malicious software introduced onto your system unknowingly
VLE	Virtual Learning Environment
VmWare	Leading supplier of virtualization software (http://www.vmware.com)
VoIP	Voice over Internet Protocol
VTCT	Vocational Training Charitable Trust (www.vtct.org.uk)
Wi-Fi	Wireless Fidelity is used to refer to wireless intercommunication between computers
Wiki	Collaborative online information resource
Wikipedia	A vast on-line encyclopaedia (http://www.wikipedia.org)
Windows	See Microsoft Windows
WJEC	Welsh Joint Education Committee (www.wjec.co.uk)
WWW	World Wide Web
Yahoo!	Popular search engine (http://www.yahoo.com)
YouTube	Popular social networking and video sharing service (http://www.youtube.com)

References

Assessment Reform Group (2002) Assessment for learning reforms. http://www.assessment-reform-group.org/CIE3.PDF (accessed 2 May 2010).

BBC (2009a) Facebook remark teenager is fired. http://news.bbc.co.uk/1/hi/england/essex/7914415.stm (accessed 30 April 2009).

BBC (2009b) Ill worker fired over Facebook. http://news.bbc.co.uk/1/hi/technology/8018329.stm (accessed 30 April 2009).

Becta (2008) *Harnessing Technology: Next Generation Learning 2008–14: A Summary* http://publications.becta.org.uk/display.cfm?resID=37346 (accessed 2 May 2010).

Beetham, H., McGill, L. and Littlejohn, A. (2009) *Thriving in the 21st century: Learning Literacies for the Digital Age (LLiDA project)*. http://www.academy.gcal.ac.uk/llida/report litreview.pdf (accessed 21 October 2009).

Brown, S. and Glasner, A. (eds) (1999) *Assessment Matters in Higher Education: Choosing and Using Diverse Approaches*. Buckingham: Open University Press.

Bunz, M. (2009) Google fined €10,000 a day for putting French books online. *The Guardian*, 19 December, p. 23.

Carr, N. (2006) Avatars use as much electricity as Brazilians. *Rough Type*, 5 December. http://www.roughtype.com/archives/2006/12/avatars_consume.php (accessed 30 August 2009).

Castells, M. (2000) *The Rise of the Network Society*, 2nd edn. Oxford: Blackwell.

Department for Business, Enterprise and Regulatory Reform (BERR) (2009). *Women in IT scorecard: a definitive up to date evidence base for data and commentary on women in IT employment and education*. http://www.e-skills.com/Research-and-policy/2535 (accessed 12 November 2009).

Department for Business, Innovation and Skills (BIS) (2009a) *Digital Britain: Final Report* (Carter), Cm. 7650. London: TSO. http://www.culture.gov.uk/images/publications/digital britain-finalreport-jun09.pdf (accessed 13 August 2009).

Department for Business, Innovation and Skills (BIS) (2009b) *Independent Review of ICT User Skills* (Morris). http://www.dius.gov.uk/~/media/3F79A51589404CFDB62F3DA0 DEBA69A1.ashx (accessed 2 May 2010).

Department for Children, Schools and Families (DCSF) (2007) *The Children's Plan*. http://www.dcsf.gov.uk/childrensplan/ (accessed 12 September 2009).

Department for Children, Schools and Families (DCSF) (2008a) *Safer Children in a Digital World: Full Report* (Byron Review). http://www.dcsf.gov.uk/byronreview (accessed 2 May 2010).

Department for Children, Schools and Families (DCSF) (2008b) *Safer Children in a Digital World: Executive Summary.* http://www.dcsf.gov.uk/byronreview/pdfs/Executive%20 summary.pdf (accessed 2 May 2010).

Department for Education and Employment (DfEE) (2001) *Skills for Life: National Strategy for Improving Adult Literacy and Numeracy Skills.* Nottingham: DfEE Publications. http:// rwp.excellencegateway.org.uk/readwriteplus/bank/ABS_Strategy_Doc_Final.pdf (accessed 22 April 2010).

Egan, R., Jefferies, P. and Stockford, A. (2009). Makeshift or marvellous: Are ICT classrooms fit for learning in the 21st Century? In I. Gibson *et al.* (eds), *Proceedings of Society for Information Technology & Teacher Education International Conference 2009* (pp. 875–877). Chesapeake, VA: AACE.

Eisenberg, M. and Berkowitz, R. (1990) *Information Problem-Solving: The Big Six Skills Approach to Library & Information Skills Instruction.* Norwood, NJ: Ablex.

E-Skills UK (2009a) *E-Skills Bulletin,* 25. http://www.e-skills.com/Research-and-policy/ bulletin/1056 (accessed 14 September 2009).

E-Skills UK (2009b) CC4G. – courseware. http://www.e-skills.com/CC4G-celebration/CC4G-courseware/2342# (accessed 10 June 2009).

E-Skills UK (2009c) e-skills internship. http://www.e-skills.com/e-skills-UK-in-work/e-skills-internship/2580 (accessed 12 December 2009).

Google Books (2009) The future of Google Books: Our groundbreaking agreement with authors and publishers. http://books.google.com/googlebooks/agreement/#3 (accessed 20 December 2009).

Health and Safety Executive (HSE) (2006) *Working with VDUs.* http://www.hse.gov.uk/pubns/ indg36.pdf (accessed 28 December 2009).

Jameson, A. (2009) School-leavers are not up to the job. *The Times Online,* 24 November. http://business.timesonline.co.uk/tol/business/management/article6928861.ece (accessed 28 November 2009).

Kuhlthau, C. (1987) *Information Skills for an Information Society: A Review of Research.* Syracuse, NY: ERIC Clearinghouse on Information Resources.

Mi2G (2005) More than 1% GDP drop estimated per week of Internet blackout. http:// www.mi2g.com/cgi/mi2g/frameset.php?pageid=http%3A//www.mi2g.com/cgi/mi2g/press/ 220705.php (accessed 15 August 2009).

Norris, P. (2001) *Digital Divide, Civic Engagement, Information Poverty and the Internet Worldwide.* Cambridge: Cambridge University Press.

Orr, D., Appleton, M., & Wallin, M. (2001) Information literacy and flexible delivery: Creating a conceptual framework and model. *Journal of Academic Librarianship,* 27(6), pp. 457–463.

Pask, G. (1975) *Conversation, Cognition and Learning.* New York: Elsevier.

Phelps, R., Ellis, A. and Hase, S. (2001) The role of metacognitive and reflective learning processes in developing capable computer users. In G. Kennedy, M. Keppell, C. McNaught & T. Petrovic (eds), *Meeting at the Crossroads.* Proceedings of the 18th Annual Conference of the Australian Society for Computers in Learning in Tertiary Education (pp. 481–490). Melbourne: Biomedical Multimedia Unit, University of Melbourne. http://www.ascilite. org.au/conferences/melbourne01/pdf/papers/phelpsr.pdf (accessed 20 December 2009).

Prensky, M. (2001) Digital natives, digital immigrants. *On the Horizon,* 9(5).

Prensky, M. (2009) H. Sapiens Digital: From digital immigrants and digital natives to digital wisdom. *Journal of Online Education,* 5(3).

Race, P. (2000) *A Briefing on Self, Peer and Group Assessment.* Assessment Series No.9, Language and Teaching Support Centre. http://www.york.ac.uk/admin/aso/learning andteaching/briefingon%20selfpeers%20and%20group%20assessmen.rtf (accessed 15 February 2010).

Saunders, D. and Race, P. (eds) (1992) *Developing and Measuring Competence: Aspects of Educational and Training Technology XXV*. London: Kogan Page.

Selwyn, N. (1997) The effect of using a computer at home on students use of IT *Research in Education*, 58, pp. 79–81.

Tummons, J. (2007) *Assessing Learning in the Lifelong Learning Sector*, 2nd edn. Exeter: Learning Matters.

Van Dijk, J. (2005) *The Deepening Divide: Inequality in the Information Society*. London: Sage Publications.

Index

Related books from Open University Press
Purchase from www.openup.co.uk or order through your local bookseller

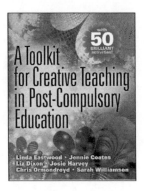

A TOOLKIT FOR CREATIVE TEACHING IN POST-COMPULSORY EDUCATION

Linda Eastwood, Jennie Coates, Liz Dixon, Josie Harvey, Chris Ormondroyd and Sarah Williamson

978-0-335-23416-5 (Paperback)
2009

eBook also available

This is the essential resource for trainees and teachers working in the PCET sector who are looking for new and creative ways of engaging and motivating their learners.

Key features:

- 50 practical and innovative teaching activities
- Variations and subject-specific examples
- Thinking Points to encourage reflection
- A theoretical framework which sets the activities within the context of creativity and innovation

www.openup.co.uk

**SUPPORTING LEARNERS IN THE
LIFELONG LEARNING SECTOR**

Marilyn Fairclough

978-0-335-23362-5 (Paperback)
2009

eBook also available

This is the first book of its kind to deal with the topic of supporting learners in PCET, rather than just focusing on how to teach them.

Key features:

- Each chapter cross-referenced to the QTLS Professional Standard for those on PTLLS, CTLLS and DTLLS courses
- Real life examples from a variety of settings and subjects
- Practical suggestions for developing classroom practice
- Suggestions for managing disruptive behaviour

www.openup.co.uk

**MODELS OF LEARNING,
TOOLS FOR TEACHING
Third Edition**

Bruce Joyce, Emily Calhoun
and David Hopkins

978-0-335-23419-6 (Paperback)
2008

eBook also available

This bestselling text provides a comprehensive and accessible
introduction to an array of models of teaching and learning.

Key features:

- A new chapter on teaching adolescents with disabilities to read
- A wealth of new scenarios and examples with clear guidelines for
  implementation
- New research and illustrations
- A revised Picture Word Inductive Model

www.openup.co.uk

 **OPEN UNIVERSITY PRESS**
McGraw - Hill Education